Writing for Journalists

Writing for Journalists is about the craft of journalistic writing: how to put one word after another so that the reader gets the message – or the joke – goes on reading and comes back for more. It is a practical guide for all those who write for newspapers, periodicals and websites, whether students, trainees or professionals.

This revised and updated edition introduces the reader to the essentials of good writing. Based on critical analysis of news stories, features and reviews from daily and weekly papers, consumer magazines, specialist trade journals and a variety of websites, *Writing for Journalists* includes:

- advice on how to start writing and how to improve and develop your style
- how to write a news story which is informative, concise and readable
- tips on feature writing from researching profiles to writing product round-ups
- how to structure and write reviews
- a new chapter on writing online copy
- a glossary of journalistic terms and suggestions for further reading.

Wynford Hicks is the author of various books on journalism and writing including *English for Journalists* (Routledge, 2007), now in its third edition, and *Quite Literally: Problem Words and How to Use Them* (Routledge, 2004).

1

Media Skills

Edited by Richard Keeble, Lincoln University
Series Advisers: Wynford Hicks and Jenny McKay

The *Media Skills* series provides a concise and thorough introduction to a rapidly changing media landscape. Each book is written by media and journalism lecturers or experienced professionals and is a key resource for a particular industry. Offering helpful advice and information and using practical examples from print, broadcast and digital media, as well as discussing ethical and regulatory issues, *Media Skills* books are essential guides for students and media professionals.

Writing for Journalists

Second edition

Wynford Hicks

with Sally Adams, Harriett Gilbert
and Tim Holmes

Routledge
Taylor & Francis Group

LONDON AND NEW YORK

First published 1999 by Routledge
2 Park Square, Milton Park, Abingdon, Oxon OX14 4RN

Simultaneously published in the USA and Canada
by Routledge
270 Madison Ave, New York, NY 10016

Reprinted 2000, 2001, 2002, 2003, 2004, 2005 (three times),
2006 (twice), 2007 (twice)

Second edition published 2008

Routledge is an imprint of the Taylor & Francis Group, an informa business

Typeset in Goudy Oldstyle by
Keystroke, 28 High Street, Tettenhall, Wolverhampton
Printed and bound in Great Britain by
TJ International Ltd, Padstow, Cornwall

British Library Cataloguing in Publication Data
A catalogue record for this book is available from the British Library

Library of Congress Cataloging in Publication Data
Hicks, Wynford, 1942–
Writing for journalists / Wynford Hicks, with Sally Adams, Harriett Gilbert
and Tim Holmes.—2nd ed.
p. cm.—(Media skills)
Includes bibliographical references and index.
1. Journalism—Authorship. I. Adams, Sally, 1933– II. Gilbert, Harriett, 1948–
III. Holmes, Tim, 1953– IV. Title.
PN4783.H53 2008
808'.06607—dc22
2007048274

ISBN10: 0–415–46020–4 (hbk)
ISBN10: 0–415–46021–2 (pbk)
ISBN10: 0–203–92710–9 (ebk)

ISBN13: 978–0–415–46020–0 (hbk)
ISBN13: 978–0–415–46021–7 (pbk)
ISBN13: 978–0–203–92710–6 (ebk)

Contents

Contributors

Wynford Hicks has worked as a reporter, subeditor, feature writer, editor and editorial consultant for newspapers, books and magazines and as a teacher of journalism specialising in writing, subediting and the use of English. He is the author of *English for Journalists*, now in its third edition, and *Quite Literally*, and co-author of *Subediting for Journalists*.

Sally Adams is a writer, editor and lecturer. She was deputy editor of *She*, editor of *Mother and Baby* and *Weight Watchers Magazine*, a reporter on the *Christchurch Press*, New Zealand, and letters page editor on the *San Francisco Chronicle*. She has written for the *Guardian*, *Daily Mail*, *Company*, *Evening Standard* and *Good Housekeeping* and is a visiting tutor at the London College of Fashion. She is the author of *Interviewing for Journalists*.

Harriett Gilbert is a novelist, broadcaster and journalist. She was literary editor of the *New Statesman* and has reviewed the arts for, among others, *Time Out*, the *Listener*, the *Independent* and the BBC. She presents *The Word* and *The World Book Club* for BBC World Service Radio. She is a senior lecturer in the Department of Journalism and Publishing at City University London where she runs the MA in Creative Writing (Novels).

Tim Holmes is a freelance journalist and former magazine publisher. He teaches and researches magazine journalism at the Centre for Journalism Studies, Cardiff University, and is the co-author of *Subediting for Journalists*.

Acknowledgements

The authors and publisher would like to thank all those journalists whose work we have quoted to illustrate the points made in this book. In particular we would like to thank the following for permission to reprint material:

'McDonald's the winner and loser'
Ian Cobain, *Daily Mail*, 20 June 1997 © *Daily Mail*

'Parson's course record puts pressure on Woods'
Daily Telegraph, 14 February 1997 © *The Daily Telegraph*

'Man killed as L-drive car plunges off cliff'
Sean O'Neill, *Daily Telegraph*, 7 January 1998 © *The Daily Telegraph*. With thanks to Sean O'Neill

'Abbey overflows for Compton'
Matthew Engel, *The Guardian*, 2 July 1997. Copyright Guardian News & Media Ltd 1997

'Picnic in the bedroom'
Janet Harmer, *Caterer and Hotelkeeper*, 11 June 1998. Reproduced with the permission of the Editor of *Caterer and Hotelkeeper*

'I love the job but do I have to wear that hat?'
Kerry Fowler, *Good Housekeeping*, June 1998. Reproduced with permission from *Good Housekeeping*, June 1998

Review of *The Whereabouts of Eneas McNulty*
Used with the permission of Adam Mars-Jones. Copyright Guardian
News & Media Ltd 1997

Review of *From the Choirgirl Hotel*
Sylvia Patterson © Frank/Wagadon Ltd

1
Introduction

WHAT THIS BOOK IS

This book is about the craft of journalistic writing: putting one word after another so that the reader gets the message – or the joke – goes on reading and comes back for more. Good writing is essential to journalism: without it important news, intriguing stories, insight and analysis, gossip and opinion could not reach their potential audience.

Writing can also be a pleasure in itself: finding the right word, getting it to fit together with other words in a sentence, constructing a paragraph that conveys meaning and creates delight . . . There is pride in a well-written piece, in the positive feedback from editors, readers, fellow journalists.

This book is a practical guide for those who write for publication, whether they are students, trainees or more experienced people. Though aimed at professionals, it should also be useful to those who write as a hobby, for propaganda purposes – or because they have a passionate love of writing.

We have revised and updated the book for this second edition. The biggest change is that it now includes a separate chapter on writing online. We have tried to concentrate our advice on online writing in this one chapter rather than making frequent references to it in the other chapters. In revising the book we have kept most of the examples of good and bad practice that were included in the first edition: there seemed little point in replacing material that remains relevant.

WHAT THIS BOOK IS NOT

This is neither a book about journalism nor a careers guide for would-be journalists. It does not set out to survey the field, to describe the various jobs that journalists do in different media. Nor is it a review of the issues in journalism. It does not discuss privacy or bias or the vexed question of the ownership of the press. It does not try to answer the question: is journalism in decline? Thus it is unlikely to be adopted as a media studies textbook.

It does not include broadcast journalism, though many of the points made also apply to TV and radio writing. It does not give detailed guidance on specialised areas such as sport, fashion, consumer and financial journalism. And it does not try to cover what might be called the public relations or propaganda sector of journalism, where getting a particular message across is the key. Magazines published by companies for their employees and customers, by charities for their donors and recipients, by trade unions and other organisations for their members – and all the other publications that are sponsored rather than market-driven – develop their own rules. Journalists who work in this sector learn to adapt to them.

Except in passing this book does not tell you how to find stories, do research or interview people.

Though subeditors – and trainee subs – should find it useful as a guide to rewriting, it does not pretend to be a sub's manual. It does not tell you how to cut copy, write headlines or check proofs. It does not cover editing, design, media law . . .

We make no apology for this. In our view writing is the key journalistic skill without which everything else would collapse. That is why we think it deserves a book of its own.

WHO CARES ABOUT WRITING?

This may look like a silly question: surely all journalists, particularly editors, aspire to write well themselves and publish good writing? Alas, apparently not. The experience of some graduates of journalism courses in their first jobs is that much of what they learnt at college is neither valued nor even wanted by their editors and senior colleagues.

Of course, this might mean that what was being taught at college, instead of being proper journalism, was some kind of ivory-tower nonsense – but the evidence is all the other way. British journalism courses are responsive to industry demands, vetted by professional training bodies – and taught by journalists.

The problem is that many editors and senior journalists don't seem to bother very much about whether their publications are well written – or even whether they are in grammatically correct English. As Harry Blamires wrote in his introduction to *Correcting your English*, a collection of mistakes published in newspapers and magazines:

> Readers may be shocked, as indeed I was myself, to discover the sheer quantity of error in current journalism. They may be astonished to find how large is the proportion of error culled from the quality press and smart magazines. Assembling the bad sentences together en masse brings home to us that we have come to tolerate a shocking degree of slovenliness and illogicality at the level of what is supposed to be educated communication.

It's true that some of what Blamires calls 'error' is conscious colloquialism but most of his examples prove his point: many editors don't seem to bother very much about the quality of the writing they publish.

Others, on the other hand, do. There is some excellent writing published in British newspapers and periodicals. And it is clear that it can help to bring commercial success. For example, the *Daily Mail* outsells the *Daily Express*, its traditional rival, for all sorts of reasons. One of them certainly is the overall quality and professionalism of the *Mail's* writing.

But if you're a trainee journalist in an office where good writing is not valued, do not despair. Do the job you're doing as well as you can – and get ready for your next one. The future is more likely to be yours than your editor's.

CAN WRITING BE TAUGHT?

This is the wrong question – unless you're a prospective teacher of journalism. The question, if you're a would-be journalist (or indeed any kind of writer), is: can writing be learnt?

And the answer is: of course it can, providing that you have at least some talent and – what is more important – that you have a lot of determination and are prepared to work hard.

If you want to succeed as a writer, you must be prepared to read a lot, finding good models and learning from them; you must be prepared to think imaginatively about readers and how they think and feel rather than luxuriate inside your own comfortable world; you must be prepared to take time practising, experimenting, revising.

You must be prepared to listen to criticism and take it into account while not letting it get on top of you. You must develop confidence in your own ability but not let it become arrogance.

This book makes all sorts of recommendations about how to improve your writing but it cannot tell you how much progress you are likely to make. It tries to be helpful and encouraging but it does not pretend to be diagnostic. And – unlike those gimmicky writing courses advertised to trap the vain, the naive and the unwary – it cannot honestly 'guarantee success or your money back'.

GETTING DOWN TO IT

Make a plan before you start

Making a plan before you start to write is an excellent idea, even if you keep it in your head. And the longer and more complex the piece, the more there is to be gained from setting the plan down on paper – or on the keyboard.

Of course you may well revise the plan as you go, particularly if you start writing before your research is completed. But that is not a reason for doing without a plan.

Write straight onto the keyboard

Unless you want to spend your whole life writing, which won't give you much time to find and research stories – never mind going to the pub or practising the cello – don't bother with a handwritten draft. Why introduce an unnecessary stage into the writing process?

Don't use the excuse that your typing is slow and inaccurate. First, obviously, learn to touch-type, so you can write straight onto the keyboard at the speed at which you think. For most people this will be about 25 words a minute – a speed far slower than that of a professional copy typist.

(There's a key distinction here between the skills of typing and shorthand. As far as writing is concerned, there's not much point in learning to type faster than 25wpm: accuracy is what counts. By contrast, the shorthand speeds that most journalism students and trainees reach if they work hard, typically 80–100wpm, are of limited use in getting down extensive quotes of normal speech. Shorthand really comes into its own above 100wpm.)

Even if you don't type very well, you should avoid the handwritten draft stage. After all, the piece is going to end up typed – presumably by you. So get down to it straightaway, however few fingers you use.

Write notes to get started

Some people find the act of writing difficult. They feel inhibited from starting to write, as though they were on a high diving board or the top of a ski run.

Reporters don't often suffer from this kind of writer's block because, assuming they have found a story in the first place, the task of writing an intro for it is usually a relatively simple one. Note: not easy but simple, meaning that reporters have a limited range of options; they are not conventionally expected to invent, to be 'creative'.

One reason why journalists should start as reporters is that it's a great way to get into the habit of writing.

However, if you've not yet acquired the habit and tend to freeze at the keyboard, don't just sit there agonising. Having written your basic plan, add further headings, enumerate, list, illustrate. Don't sweat over the first paragraph: begin somewhere in the middle; begin with something you know you're going to include, like an anecdote or a quote. You can reposition it later. Get started, knowing that on the keyboard you're not committed to your first draft.

Revise, revise

Always leave yourself time to revise what you have written. Even if you're writing news to a tight deadline, try to spend a minute or two looking over your story. And if you're a feature writer or reviewer, revision is an essential part of the writing process.

If you're lucky, a competent subeditor will check your copy before it goes to press, but that is no reason to pretend to yourself that you are not responsible for what you write. As well as looking for the obvious – errors of fact, names wrong, spelling and grammar mistakes, confusion caused by bad punctuation – try to read your story from the reader's point of view. Does it make sense in their terms? Is it clear? Does it really hit the target?

Master the basics

You can't start to write well without having a grasp of the basics of English usage such as grammar, spelling and punctuation. To develop a journalistic style you will need to learn how to use quotes, handle reported speech, choose the right word from a variety of different ones. When should you use foreign words and phrases, slang, jargon – and what about clichés? What is 'house style'? And so on.

The basics of English and journalistic language are covered in a companion volume, *English for Journalists*. In this book we have in general tried not to repeat material included there.

DIFFERENT KINDS OF PRINT JOURNALISM

There are obviously different kinds of print journalism – thus different demands on the journalist as writer. Conventionally, people distinguish in market-sector terms between newspapers and periodicals, between upmarket (previously 'broadsheet') and downmarket (previously 'tabloid') papers, between consumer and business-to-business (from now on in this book called 'b2b') periodicals, and so on.

Some of these conventional assumptions can be simplistic when applied to the way journalism is written. For example, a weekly b2b periodical is in fact a newspaper. In its approach to news writing it has as much in common with other weeklies – local newspapers, say, or Sunday newspapers – as it does with monthly b2b periodicals. Indeed 'news' in monthly publications is not the same thing at all.

Second, while everybody goes on about the stylistic differences between the top and bottom ends of the newspaper market, less attention is paid to those between mid-market tabloids, such as the *Mail*, and the redtops, such as the Sun. Whereas features published by the *Guardian* are occasionally reprinted by the *Mail* (and vice versa) with no alterations to the text, most *Mail* features would not fit easily into the *Sun*.

Third, in style terms there are surprising affinities that cross the conventional divisions. For example, the *Sun* and the *Guardian* both include more jokes in the text and more punning headlines than the *Mail* does. Fourth, while *Guardian* stories typically have longer words, sentences and paragraphs than those in the *Mail*, which are in turn longer than those in the *Sun*, it does not follow, for example, that students and trainees who want to end up on the *Guardian* should practise writing at great length.

Indeed our advice to students and trainees is not to begin by imitating the style of a particular publication – or even a particular type of publication. Instead we think you should try to develop an effective writing style by learning from the various good models available. We think that – whoever you are – you can learn from good newspapers and periodicals, whether upmarket or downmarket, daily, weekly or monthly.

This book does not claim to give detailed guidance on all the possible permutations of journalistic writing. Instead we take the old-fashioned view that journalism students and trainees should gain a basic all-round competence in news and feature writing.

Thus we cover the straight news story and a number of variations, but not foreign news as such, since trainees are unlikely to find themselves being sent to Iraq or Afghanistan. Also, as has already been said, we do not set out to give detailed guidance on specialist areas such as financial and sports reporting. In features we concentrate on the basic formats used in newspapers, consumer magazines and the b2b press.

And we include a chapter on reviewing because it is not a branch of feature writing but a separate skill which is in great demand. Reviews are written by all sorts of journalists including juniors and 'experts' who often start with little experience of writing for publication.

We have taken examples from a wide range of publications and websites but we repeat: our intention is not to 'cover the field of journalism'. In newspapers we have often used examples from the nationals rather than regional or local papers because they are more familiar to readers and easier to get hold of. In periodicals, too, we have tended to use the bigger, better-known titles.

ONLINE JOURNALISM

Does writing online require a brand-new set of techniques or merely the adaptation of traditional ones? Chapter 5 on writing online discusses how the basic writing skills apply – but need to be supplemented by new ones specific to the medium.

STYLE

In the chapters that follow the different demands of writing news, features and reviews – and writing online – are discussed separately. In the final chapter we look at style as such. We review what the experts have said about the principles of good journalistic writing and suggest how you can develop an effective style.

For whatever divides the different forms of journalism there is such a thing as a distinctive journalistic approach to writing. Journalism – at least in the Anglo-Saxon tradition – is informal rather than formal; active rather than passive; a temporary, inconclusive, ad hoc, interim reaction rather than a definitive, measured statement.

Journalists always claim to deliver the latest – but never claim to have said or written the last word.

Journalism may be factual or polemical, universal or personal, laconic or ornate, serious or comic, but on top of the obvious mix of information and entertainment its stock in trade is shock, surprise, contrast. That is why journalists are always saying 'BUT', often for emphasis at the beginning of sentences.

All journalists tell stories, whether interesting in themselves or used to grab the reader's attention or illustrate a point. Journalists almost always prefer analogy (finding another example of the same thing) to analysis (breaking something down to examine it).

Journalists – in print as well as broadcasting – use the spoken word all the time. They quote what people say to add strength and colour to observation and they often use speech patterns and idioms in their writing.

Journalists are interpreters between specialist sources and the general public, translators of scientific jargon into plain English, scourges of obfuscation, mystification, misinformation. Or they should be.

A good journalist can always write a story short even if they would prefer to have the space for an expanded version. Thus the best general writing exercise for a would-be journalist is what English teachers call the precis or summary, in which a prose passage is reduced to a prescribed length. Unlike the simplest form of subediting, in which whole paragraphs are cut from a story so that its style remains unaltered, the precis involves condensing and rewriting as well as cutting.

Journalists have a confused and ambivalent relationship with up-to-date slang, coinages, trendy expressions. They are always looking for new, arresting ways of saying the same old things – but they do more than anybody else to ensure that the new quickly becomes the familiar. Thus good journalists are always trying (and often failing) to avoid clichés.

Politicians, academics and other people who take themselves far too seriously sometimes criticise journalism for being superficial. In other words, they seem to be saying, without being deep it is readable. From the writing point of view this suggests that it has hit the target.

2
Writing news

WHAT IS NEWS?

News is easy enough to define. To be news, something must be factual, new and interesting.

There must be facts to report – without them there can be no news. The facts must be new – to your readers at least. And these facts must be likely to interest your readers.

So if a historian makes a discovery about the eating habits of the ancient Britons, say, somebody can write a news story about it for the periodical *History Today*. The information will be new to its readers, though the people concerned lived hundreds of years ago. Then, when the story is published, it can be followed up by a national newspaper like the *Daily Telegraph* or the *Sunday Mirror*, on the assumption that it would appeal to their readers.

Being able to identify what will interest readers is called having a news sense. There are all sorts of dictums about news (some of which contradict others): that bad news sells more papers than good news; that news is what somebody wants to suppress; that readers are most interested in events and issues that affect them directly; that news is essentially about people; that readers want to read about people like themselves; that readers are, above all, fascinated by the lives, loves and scandals of the famous . . .

It may sound cynical but the most useful guidance for journalism students and trainees is probably that news is what's now being published on the news pages of newspapers and magazines. In other words, whatever the guides and textbooks may say, what the papers actually say is more important.

Some commentators have distinguished between 'hard' news about 'real', 'serious', 'important' events affecting people's lives and 'soft' news about 'trivial' incidents (such as a cat getting stuck up a tree and being rescued by the fire brigade). Those analysing the content of newspapers for its own sake may find this distinction useful, but in terms of journalistic style it can be a dead end. The fact is that there is no clear stylistic distinction between 'hard' and 'soft' news writing.

It makes more sense to say that there is a mainstream, traditional approach to news writing – with a number of variants. The reporter may use one of these variants – the narrative style, say – to cover the rescue of a cat stuck up a tree or an exchange of fire in Afghanistan. Or they may decide, in either case, to opt for the traditional approach. In fact both 'hard' and 'soft' news can be written either way.

Since we're talking definitions, why is a news report called a 'story'? Elsewhere, the word means anecdote or narrative, fiction or fib – though only a cynic would say that the last two definitions tell the essential truth about journalism.

In fact the word 'story' applied to a news report emphasises that it is a construct, something crafted to interest a reader (rather than an unstructured 'objective' version of the facts). In some ways the word is misleading since, as we shall see, a traditional news story does not use the narrative style.

And, while we're at it, what is an 'angle'? As with 'story' the dictionary seems to provide ammunition for those hostile to journalism. An angle is 'a point of view, a way of looking at something (*informal*); a scheme, a plan devised for profit (*slang*)', while to angle is 'to present (news, etc) in such a way as to serve a particular end' (*Chambers Dictionary*, 10th edition, 2006).

We can't blame the dictionary for jumbling things together but there is a key distinction to be made between having a way of looking at something (essential if sense is to be made of it) and presenting news to serve a particular purpose (propaganda). Essentially, a news angle comes from the reporter's interpretation of events – which they invite the reader to share.

> McDonald's won a hollow victory over two Green campaigners yesterday after the longest libel trial in history.
> *Daily Mail*

The word 'hollow', particularly combined with 'longest', shows that the reporter has a clear idea of what the story is. Advocates of 'objective' journalism may criticise this 'reporting from a point of view' – but nowadays all national papers do it.

> Victims of the world's worst *E coli* food poisoning outbreak reacted furiously last night after the Scottish butcher's shop which sold contaminated meat was fined just £2,250.
> *Guardian*

That 'just' shows clearly what the reporter thinks of the fine.

A QUICK WORD BEFORE YOU START

It's not original to point out that news journalism is all about questions: the ones you ask yourself before you leave the office or pick up the phone; the ones you ask when you're interviewing and gathering material – above all, the ones your reader wants you to answer.

Begin with the readers of your publication. You need to know who they are, what they're interested in, what makes them tick. (For more on this see 'Writing features', pages 47–9.)

Then what's the story about? In some cases – a fire, say – the question answers itself. In others – a complicated fraud case – you may have to wrestle with the material to make it make sense.

Never be afraid to ask the news editor or a senior colleague if you're confused about what you're trying to find out. Better a moment's embarrassment before you start than the humiliation of realising, after you've written your story, that you've been missing the point all along. The same applies when you're interviewing. Never be afraid to ask apparently obvious questions – if you have to.

The trick, though, is to be well briefed – and then ask your questions. Try to know more than a reporter would be expected to know. But don't parade your knowledge: ask your questions in a straightforward way. Challenge when necessary, probe certainly, interrupt if you have to – but never argue when you're interviewing. Be polite, firm, controlled, professional. It may sound old-fashioned but you represent your publication and its readers.

Routine is vital to news gathering. Always read your own publication – and its rivals – regularly; maintain your contacts book and diary;

remember to ask people their ages if that is what the news editor insists on. Above all, when interviewing, get people's names right. Factual accuracy is vital to credible news journalism. A bright and clever story is worse than useless if its content is untrue: more people will read it – and more people will be misinformed.

NEWS FORMULAS

The two most commonly quoted formulas in the traditional approach to news writing are Rudyard Kipling's six questions (sometimes abbreviated to the five Ws) and the news pyramid (usually described as 'inverted').

The six questions

Kipling's six questions – who, what, how, where, when, why – provide a useful checklist for news stories, and it's certainly possible to write an intro that includes them all. The textbook example is:

> Lady Godiva (WHO) rode (WHAT) naked (HOW) through the streets of Coventry (WHERE) yesterday (WHEN) in a bid to cut taxes (WHY).

This is facetiously called the clothesline intro – because you can hang everything on it. There is nothing wrong with this particular example but there is no reason why every news intro should be modelled on it. Indeed some intros would become very unwieldy if they tried to answer all six questions.

In general, the six questions should all be answered somewhere in the story – but there are exceptions. For example, in a daily paper a reporter may have uncovered a story several days late. They will try to support it with quotes obtained 'yesterday'; but there is no point in emphasising to readers that they are getting the story late. So the exact date on which an event took place should not be given unless it is relevant.

In weekly papers and periodicals 'this week' may be relevant; 'last week' as a regular substitute for the daily paper's 'yesterday' is usually pointless. Even worse is 'recently', which carries a strong whiff of staleness and amateurism – best left to the club newsletter and the parish magazine.

So the six questions should be kept as a checklist. When you've written a news story, check whether you've failed to answer one of the questions –

and so weakened your story. But if there is no point in answering a particular question, don't bother with it.

Two of these questions – who and what – are obviously essential. In all news intros somebody or something must do or experience something. A useful distinction can be made between 'who' stories, in which the focus is on the person concerned, and 'what' stories, which are dominated by what happens. As we shall see, drawing this distinction can help you decide whether or not to include a person's name in an intro.

The news pyramid

This particular pyramid is not quite as old as the ancient Egyptians. But as a formula for analysing, teaching and practising news writing it goes back a long way. And the pyramid is certainly a useful idea (the only mystery is why most commentators insist on 'inverting' it – turning it upside down – when it does the job perfectly well the right way up). The purpose of the pyramid is to show that the points in a news story are made in descending order of importance. News is written so that readers can stop reading when they have satisfied their curiosity – without worrying that something important is being held back. To put it another way, news is written so that subeditors can cut stories from the bottom up – again, without losing something important.

As we shall see, some stories don't fit the pyramid idea as well as others – but it remains a useful starting point for news writing.

INTROS 1: TRADITIONAL

The news intro should be able to stand on its own. Usually one sentence, it conveys the essence of the story in a clear, concise, punchy way: general enough to be understood; precise enough to be distinguished from other stories.

It should contain few words – usually fewer than 30, often fewer than 20.

First, decide what your story is about: like any other sentence a news intro has a subject. Then ask yourself two questions: why this story now? And how would you start telling your reader the story if you met them in the pub?

The intro is your chance to grab your reader's attention so that they read the story. If you fail, the whole lot goes straight in the bin.

The intro should make sense instantly to your reader. Often it should say how the story will affect them, what it means in practice. And always prefer the concrete to the abstract.

- Don't start with questions or with things that need to be explained – direct quotes, pronouns, abbreviations (except the most common).
- Don't start with things that create typographical problems – figures, italics, direct quotes again.
- Don't start with things that slow the sentence – subordinate clauses, participles, parentheses, long, difficult, foreign words.
- Don't start with when and where, how and why.
- Do start with a crisp sentence in clear English that tells the whole story vividly.

When you've written the whole story, go back and polish your intro; then see if you can use it to write a working news headline. That will tell you whether you've still got more work to do.

Who or what?

If everybody were equal in news terms, all intros might be general and start: 'A man', 'A company', 'A football team'. Alternatively, they might all be specific and start: 'Gordon Brown'/'John Evans'; 'ICI'/'Evans Hairdressing'; 'Arsenal'/'Brize Norton Rangers'.

Between 'A man' and 'Gordon Brown'/'John Evans' there are various steps: 'A Scottish MP' is one; 'A New Labour minister'/'An Islington hairdresser' another. Then there's the explaining prefix that works as a title: 'New Labour leader Gordon Brown'/'Islington hairdresser John Evans' (though some upmarket papers still refuse to use this snappy 'tabloid' device).

But the point is that people are not equally interesting in news terms. Some are so well known that their name is enough to sell a story, however trivial. Others will only get into the paper by winning the national lottery or dying in a car crash.

Here is a typical WHO intro about a celebrity – without his name there would be no national paper story:

> Comic Eddie Izzard fought back when he was attacked in the street
> by an abusive drunk, a court heard yesterday.
> *Daily Mail*

Note the contrast with:

> A crown court judge who crashed his Range Rover while five times
> over the drink-drive limit was jailed for five months yesterday.
> *Daily Telegraph*

A crown court judge he may be – but not many *Telegraph* readers would recognise his name: it is his occupation not his name that makes this a front-page story.

And finally the anonymous figure 'A man' – his moment of infamy is entirely due to what he has done:

> A man acquitted of murder was convicted yesterday of harassing
> the family of a police officer who helped investigate him.
> *Guardian*

So the first question to ask yourself in writing an intro is whether your story is essentially WHO or WHAT: is the focus on the person or on what they've done? This helps to answer the question: does the person's name go in the intro or is their identification delayed to the second or third par?

Local papers tend to have stories about 'an Islington man' where the nationals prefer 'a hairdresser' and b2b papers go straight to 'top stylist John Evans'. On the sports page both locals and nationals use 'Arsenal' and their nickname 'the Gunners' (or 'Gooners'). In their own local paper Brize Norton Rangers may be 'Rangers'; but when they play Arsenal in the FA Cup, to everybody else they have to become something like 'the non-League club Brize Norton' or 'non-Leaguers Brize Norton'.

When?

There is an exception to the general rule that you shouldn't begin by answering the WHEN question:

> Two years after merchant bank Barings collapsed with £830m
> losses, it is back in hot water.
> *Daily Mail*

If starting this way gives the story a strong angle, by all means do it. (And the same argument could apply to WHERE, HOW and WHY – but such occasions are rare.)

After

'After' is a useful way of linking two stages of a story without having to say 'because'. Always use 'after' rather than 'following' to do this: it is shorter, clearer – and not journalistic jargon.

> A Cambridge student who killed two friends in a drunken car crash left court a free man yesterday after a plea for clemency from one of the victims' parents.
> *Guardian*

In this case the judge may have been influenced by the plea for clemency – but even if he was, that would still not enable the reporter to say 'because'.

> A woman artist was on the run last night after threatening to shoot three judges in the Royal Courts of Justice.
> *Daily Mail*

Here the first part of the intro is an update on the second.

In some stories the 'after' links the problem with its solution:

> A six-year-old boy was rescued by firemen after he became wedged under a portable building being used as a polling station.
> *Daily Telegraph*

In others the 'after' helps to explain the first part of the intro:

> An aboriginal man was yesterday speared 14 times in the legs and beaten on the head with a nulla nulla war club in a traditional punishment after Australia's courts agreed to recognise tribal justice.
> *Guardian*

Sometimes 'after' seems too weak to connect the two parts of an intro:

> Examiners were accused of imposing a 'tax on Classics' yesterday after announcing they would charge sixth formers extra to take A-levels in Latin and Greek.
> *Daily Mail*

It is certainly true that A happened after B – but it also happened because of B. There should be a stronger link between the two parts of the intro.

One point or two?

As far as possible, intros should be about one point not two, and certainly not several. The double intro can sometimes work:

> Bill Clinton has completed his selection of the most diverse Cabinet in US history by appointing the country's first woman law chief.
>
> The President-elect also picked a fourth black and a second Hispanic to join his top team.
> *Daily Mail*

Here the *Mail* reporter (or sub) has divided the intro into two separate pars. It's easier to read this way.

> Australian Lucas Parsons equalled the course record with a nine-under-par 64, but still could not quite take the spotlight away from Tiger Woods in the first round of the Australian Masters in Melbourne yesterday.
> *Daily Telegraph*

Yes, it's a bit long but the reporter just gets away with it. Everybody is expecting to read about current hero Tiger Woods but here's this sensation – a course record by a little-known golfer.

In some stories the link between two points is so obvious that a concise double intro is probably the only way to go. In the two examples below 'both' makes the point:

> Battersea's boxing brothers Howard and Gilbert Eastman both maintained their undefeated professional records at the Elephant and Castle Leisure Centre last Saturday.
> *Wandsworth Borough Guardian*

> Loftus Road – owner of Queens Park Rangers – and Sheffield United both announced full-year operating losses.
> *Guardian*

(Obvious or not, the link does give problems in developing the story – see 'Splitting the pyramid,' pages 33–5.)

The main cause of clutter in news stories is trying to say too much in the intro. This makes the intro itself hard to read – and the story hard to develop clearly. Here is a cluttered intro:

> Marketing junk food to children has to become socially unaccept-able, a leading obesity expert will say today, warning that the food industry has done too little voluntarily to help avert what a major report this week will show is a 'far worse scenario than even our gloomiest predictions'.
> *Guardian*

The problem here is that the reporter wants to link two apparently unconnected statements on the same subject – which is fair enough in the story but certainly not in the intro where it can only confuse. The natural place to end the intro is after 'will say today'. That would leave it clear and concise.

Instead the sentence meanders on with the 'warning' followed by the doom-laden 'major report'. But what's being asserted is not 'warning' at all – 'warning' here is journalese for saying/claiming etc. Then there's the word 'voluntarily' – which adds nothing to 'done too little'; there's 'help' – which is unnecessary; there's 'major' – journalese again (whoever heard of a 'minor' report?); and there's the word 'show', which implies endorse-ment of the report's findings instead of merely describing them. Finally we get to the 'scenario' and the gloomy predictions.

A sentence that starts with a simple message in clear ordinary language – 'stop marketing junk food to children' – degenerates into clumsily expressed, convoluted jargon.

As and when

'As' is often used in intros to link two events that occur at the same time:

> A National Lottery millionaire was planning a lavish rerun of her wedding last night as a former colleague claimed she was being denied her rightful share of the jackpot.
> *Daily Telegraph*

This approach rarely works. Here the main point of the story is not A (the planned second wedding) but B (the dispute) – as is shown by the fact that the next 10 pars develop it; the 11th par covers the wedding plans; and the final four pars return to the dispute.

In contrast to 'as', 'when' is often used for intros that have two bites at the cherry: the first grabs the reader's attention; the second justifies the excitement:

> A crazed woman sparked panic in the High Court yesterday when she burst in and held a gun to a judge's head.
> *Sun*

> A naive Oxford undergraduate earned a double first from the university of life when he was robbed by two women in one day, a court heard today.
> London *Evening Standard*

Specific or summary?

Should an intro begin with an example, then generalise – or make a general statement, then give an example? Should it be specific – or summary/portmanteau/comprehensive?

> Torrential rain in Spain fell mainly on the lettuces last month – and it sent their prices rocketing.
> *Guardian*

This intro to a story on retail price inflation grabs the attention in a way that a general statement would not. Whenever possible, choose a specific news point rather than a general statement for your intro.

But weather reports can be exceptions. Here's the first par of a winter weather story:

> The first snowfalls of winter brought much of the South East to a standstill today after temperatures plunged below freezing. The wintry onslaught claimed its first victim when a motorist was killed in Kent.
> London *Evening Standard*

Pity about 'plunged' and 'wintry onslaught' – they were probably in the cuttings for last year's snow story too. But otherwise the intro works well for the *Standard*, which covers much of the south east around London. A Kent paper would have led on the death.

The wider the area your paper covers the greater the argument for a general intro on a weather story.

Fact or claim?

This is a vital distinction in news. Are you reporting something as fact – or reporting that somebody has said something in a speech or a written report? An avalanche of news comes by way of reports and surveys; courts, councils and tribunals; public meetings and conferences.

In these stories you must attribute – say who said it – in the intro. Tabloids sometimes delay the attribution to the second or third par – but this practice is not recommended: it risks confusion in the reader's mind.

> Skiers jetting off for the slopes are risking a danger much worse than broken bones, according to university research published today.
> *Guardian*

Note that this is a general not a detailed attribution – that comes later in the story. Only give a name in the intro when it is likely to be recognised by the reader.

The WHO/WHAT distinction is important in these stories. The rule is to start with what is said – unless the person saying it is well known, as in:

> Sir Jackie Stewart, the former motor-racing world champion, has accused his fellow Scots of being lazy and overdependent on public sector 'jobs for life'.
> *Sunday Times*

If your story is based on a speech or written report you give the detail (eg WHERE) lower in the story. But if it is based on a press conference or routine interview, there is no need to mention this. Writing 'said at a press conference' or 'said in a telephone interview' is like nudging the reader and saying 'I'm a journalist, really'.

Some publications, particularly b2b periodicals, are inclined to parade the fact that they have actually interviewed somebody for a particular news story, as in 'told the *Muckshifters' Gazette*'. This is bad style because it suggests that on other occasions no interview has taken place – that the publication's news stories are routinely based on unchecked press releases. Where this is standard practice, it is stretching a point to call it 'news writing'.

Past, present – or future?

Most news intros report what happened, so are written in the past tense. But some are written in the present tense, which is more immediate, more vivid to the reader:

> An advert for Accurist watches featuring an ultra-thin model is being investigated by the Advertising Standards Authority.
> *Guardian*

News of the investigation makes a better intro than the fact that people have complained to the ASA: as well as being more immediate it takes the story a stage further.

Some intros combine the present tense for the latest stage in the story with the past tense for the facts that grab the attention:

> BT is tightening up its telephone security system after its confidential list of ex-directory numbers was penetrated – by a woman from Ruislip.
> *Observer*

This intro also illustrates two other points: the use of AFTER to link two stages of a story (see above) and THE ELEMENT OF SURPRISE (see over). The dash emphasises the point that this huge and powerful organisation was apparently outwitted by a mere individual.

Speech-report intros are often written with the first part in the present tense and the second in the past:

> Copyright is freelances' work and they must never give it away, said Carol Lee, who is coordinating the NUJ campaign against the *Guardian*'s new rights offensive.
> *Journalist*

Note that the first part of the intro is not a quote. Quotes are not used in good news intros for two main reasons: as Harold Evans noted back in 1972,

> Offices where intros are still set with drop caps usually ban quote intros because of the typographical complications. There is more against them than that. The reader has to do too much work. He has to find out who is speaking and he may prefer to move on.

Drop caps in news intros (and male pronouns) aren't as common as they were – but the rule holds good: don't make the reader do too much work.

When you write the intro for a speech report, take the speaker's main point and, if necessary, put it in your own words. Thus the version you end up with may or may not be the actual words of the speaker. In this example we don't know what Carol Lee's words were – but they could have been more elaborate.

Here, the editing process could have gone further. A more concise version of the intro would be:

> Freelances must never give up copyright, said Carol Lee . . .

Some present-tense intros look forward to the future:

> Yule Catto, the chemicals group, is believed to be preparing a £250m bid for Holliday Chemical, its sector rival.
> *Sunday Times*

And some intros are actually written in the future tense:

> More than 1,000 travel agency shops will unite this week to become the UK's largest high street package holiday chain, using the new name WorldChoice.
> *Observer*

Where possible, use the present or the future tense rather than the past and, if you're making a prediction, be as definite as you can safely be.

The element of surprise

> A woman who fell ill with a collapsed lung on a Boeing 747 had her life saved by two doctors who carried out an operation with a coathanger, a bottle of mineral water, brandy and a knife and fork.
> *Guardian*

> Two British doctors carried out a life-saving operation aboard a jumbo jet – with a coat hanger.
> *Daily Mail*

> A doctor saved a mum's life in a mid-air operation – using a coathanger, pen top, brandy and half a plastic bottle.
> *Sun*

These three intros agree with one another more than they disagree: a woman's life was saved in mid-air by doctors using what lay to hand including a coathanger.

The best way of writing the intro puts the human drama first but does not leave the intriguing aspect of the means used until later in the story. That would risk the reader saying 'Good but so what?' – and going on to something else.

Nor in this kind of story should you begin with the bizarre. 'A coathanger, pen top, brandy and half a plastic bottle were used in an emergency midair operation . . .' misplaces the emphasis. In any newspaper the fact that a woman's life was saved comes first.

The three intros quoted above show various strengths and weaknesses: the *Guardian* is longwinded and clumsy, though accurate and informative; the *Mail* is concise, but is 'a jumbo jet' better than 'a Boeing 747' (in the intro who cares what make of plane it was?) and why just a coathanger – what happened to the brandy? The *Sun* spares us the planespotter details but insists on calling the woman 'a mum' (while failing to mention her children anywhere in the story).

And is the story mainly about a woman (*Guardian*), a doctor (*Sun*) or two British doctors (*Mail*)?

But in style the biggest contrast here is between the approach of the *Mail* and the *Sun* which both signal the move from human drama to bizarre detail by using the dash – and that of the *Guardian* which does not.

When you start with an important fact, then want to stress an unusual or surprising aspect of the story in the same sentence, the natural way to do this is with the dash. It corresponds exactly with the way you would pause and change your tone of voice in telling the story.

The running story

When a story runs from day to day it would irritate the reader to keep talking about 'A man' in the intro. Also it would be pointless: most readers either read the paper regularly or follow the news in some other way. But it is essential that each news story as a whole should include necessary background for new readers.

> The tiger which bit a circus worker's arm off was the star of the famous Esso TV commercial.
> London *Evening Standard*

After this intro the story gives an update on the victim's condition and repeats details of the accident.

Court reports are often running stories. Here the trick is to write an intro that works for both sets of readers: it should be both vivid and informative.

> The 10-year-old girl alleged to have been raped by classmates in a primary school toilet said yesterday that she just wanted to be a 'normal kid'.
> Guardian

In some cases phrases like 'renewed calls' or 'a second death' make the point that this is one more stage in a continuing drama:

> Another Catholic man was shot dead in Belfast last night just as the IRA issued a warning that the peace process in Northern Ireland was on borrowed time.
> Guardian

The follow-up

Like the running story, the follow-up should not start 'A man' if the original story is likely to be remembered. In the following example the 'mystery businessman' has enjoyed a second expensive meal weeks after the first – but the story is his identity. His name is given in par three.

> The mystery businessman who spent more than £13,000 on a dinner for three in London is a 34-year-old Czech financier who manages a £300m fortune.
> Sunday Times

INTROS 2: VARIATION

The possible variations are endless: any feature-writing technique can be applied to news writing – if it works. But two variations are particularly common: selling the story and the narrative style. The narrative sometimes turns into the delayed drop (see below).

Selling the story

Here a selling intro is put in front of a straight news story:

> If you have friends or relations in High Street banking, tell them – warn them – to find another job. Within five years, the Internet is going to turn their world upside down.

> This is the confident forecast in a 200-page report . . .
> Daily Mail

The report's forecast is that the internet will turn the world of banking upside down – that is where the straight news story starts. But the *Mail* reporter has added an intro that dramatises the story and says what it will mean in practice – for people like the reader.

> They were the jeans that launched (or relaunched) a dozen pop songs.
>
> Now Levis, the clothing manufacturer that used to turn everything it touched into gold, or even platinum, has fallen on harder times.
>
> Yesterday the company announced that it is to cut its North American workforce by a third.
> *Guardian*

The straight news in par three follows an intro that gives the story a nostalgic flavour: the reader is brought into it and reminded of their pleasurable past buying jeans and listening to pop music.

The risk with this kind of selling intro is that some readers may be turned off by it: they may not have friends in retail banking; they may not feel nostalgic about jeans and pop music. What is important here is knowing your readers and how they are likely to react.

The narrative style

Here the traditional news story approach gives way to the kind of narrative technique used in fiction:

> The thud of something falling to the ground stopped Paul Hallett in his tracks as he tore apart the rafters of an old outside lavatory.
>
> The handyman brushed off his hands and picked up a dusty wallet, half expecting to find nothing inside.
>
> But picking through the contents one by one, Mr Hallett realised he had stumbled upon the details of a US Air Force chaplain stationed at a nearby RAF base in Suffolk 50 years earlier.
> *Daily Mail*

> Choral scholar Gavin Rogers-Ball was dying for a cigarette. Stuck on a coach bringing the Wells Cathedral choir back from a performance in Germany, he had an idea – ask one of the boys to be sick

and the adult members of the choir could step off the bus for a smoke.

It was a ruse that was to cost the alto dear . . .
Guardian

Both stories begin with a dramatic moment – and name their main character. As with fiction the trick is to get the reader involved with that person and what happens to them.

News stories about court cases and tribunals can often be handled in this way, and so can any light or humorous subject. But for the technique to work there must be a story worth telling.

If you can, try to avoid the awkward use of variation words to describe your main character. 'Alto' in the *Guardian* story is particularly clumsy. (See 'Variation' on pages 37–8.)

The delayed drop

Here the story is written in narrative style and what would be the first point in a conventional intro – the real news, if you like – is kept back for effect. The change of direction is sometimes signalled by a 'BUT':

A pint-sized Dirty Harry, aged 11, terrorised a school when he pulled out a Magnum revolver in the playground. Screaming children fled in panic as the boy, who could hardly hold the powerful handgun, pointed it at a teacher.

But headmaster Arthur Casson grabbed the boy and discovered that the gun – made famous by Clint Eastwood in the film *Dirty Harry* – was only a replica.
Mirror

A naughty nurse called Janet promised kinky nights of magic to a married man who wrote her passionate love letters.

He was teased with sexy photographs, steamy suggestions and an offer to meet her at a hotel.

But soon he was being blackmailed . . . the girl of his dreams was really a man called Brian.
Mirror

As entertainment a well-told delayed-drop story is hard to beat.

STRUCTURE

News is all about answering questions – the reader's. The best guide to developing a news story is to keep asking yourself: what does the reader need or want to know now?

1 Building the pyramid

First the intro must be amplified, extended, explained, justified. For example, in a WHAT story where the main character is not named in the intro, the reader needs to know something more about them: certainly their name, probably their age and occupation, perhaps other details depending on the story. A CLAIM story where the intro gives only a general attribution – 'according to a survey' – needs a detailed attribution later on.

These are obvious, routine and in a sense formal points. Similarly, a sport story needs the score, a court story details of the charges, and so on.

A common development of a news intro in the classic news pyramid is to take the story it contains and retell it in greater detail:

Intro

> A six-year-old boy was rescued by firemen after he became wedged under a portable building being used as a polling station.

Retelling of intro

> Jack Moore was playing with friends near his home in Nevilles Cross Road, Hebburn, South Tyneside, when curiosity got the better of him and he crawled into the eight-inch space under the building, where he became firmly wedged.

> Firemen used airbags to raise the cabin before Jack was freed . . .

Further information and quote

> . . . and taken to hospital, where he was treated for cuts and bruising and allowed home. His mother, Lisa, said: 'He is a little shaken and bruised but apart from that he seems all right.'
> *Daily Telegraph*

In a longer story the intro can be retold twice, each time with more detail:

Intro

A woman artist was on the run last night after threatening to shoot three judges in the Royal Courts of Justice.

First retelling of intro

Annarita Muraglia, who is in her early 20s, stood up in the public gallery brandishing what appeared to be a Luger and ran towards the judges screaming: 'If anybody moves I am going to shoot.'

Two judges tried to reason with her as the third calmly left court 7 to raise the alarm.

Within minutes armed response units and police dog handlers surrounded the huge Victorian gothic building. But Muraglia, who has twice been jailed for contempt in the past – for stripping in court and throwing paint at a judge – disappeared into the warren of corridors.

The drama brought chaos to central London for five hours as roads around the Strand were closed. As hundreds of court staff were evacuated an RAF helicopter was drafted in to help 80 police on the ground.

Second retelling of intro

Witnesses said Lord Justice Beldam, 71, Mrs Justice Bracewell, 62, and Mr Justice Mance, 54, were hearing a routine criminal appeal when Muraglia – who had no connection with the case – stood up in the gallery.

'She was holding a gun American-style with both hands and seemed deranged,' said barrister Tom MacKinnon. 'She told the judges: "I demand you hear my case right now or I will start shooting."

'Mrs Justice Bracewell tried to reason with her but the woman started waving the gun, threatening to shoot anybody who moved.'

Lord Justice Beldam, one of the most senior High Court judges, calmly urged her to put down her gun as members of the public and lawyers sat in stunned silence.

Senior court registrar Roy Armstrong bravely approached her and asked for details of her case, but she then fled through a door to the judges' chambers.

Further information: background

Italy-born Muraglia, from Islington, North London, was jailed for contempt in December 1994 after breaking furniture and attacking staff at a child custody hearing.

Later, during a review of her sentence, she dropped her trousers to reveal her bare bottom painted with the words 'Happy Christmas'.

In July 1995, she sprayed green paint over the wig of Judge Andrew Brooks. The following month when he sentenced her to 15 months for contempt she again bared her bottom and was escorted away screaming: 'So you don't want to see my bottom again, Wiggy?'

Further information: update

Police said last night that they did not know if the gun was real or fake. They were confident of making an arrest.
Daily Mail

Alternatively, the intro may be followed by information on events leading up to it before the intro is restated:

Intro

Comic Eddie Izzard fought back when he was attacked in the street by an abusive drunk, a court heard yesterday.

Events leading up to intro

The award-winning comedian, who wears skirts and make-up on stage, had been taunted by jobless Matthew Dodkin after a stand-up show at the Corn Exchange, Cambridge, last November. Magistrates in the city heard that 22-year-old Dodkin had put his hands on his waist while running his tongue round his lips and saying: 'Ooh, Tracy.'

Mr Izzard admitted: 'I was very abusive towards him and I said he deserved to be cut with a knife.' . . .

Retelling of intro

. . . Dodkin then attacked him. 'I punched back and I struck blows, which is surprising because the last fight I had I was 12,' said Mr Izzard, 35, who suffered a cut lip and a black eye.

Further information

Dodkin, of Queensway Flats, Cambridge, declined to give evidence after denying common assault. He was fined £120 and ordered to pay £100 compensation.
Daily Mail

The intro may be followed by explanation – of a single aspect of the intro or of the intro as a whole:

Intro

> An advert for Accurist watches featuring an ultra-thin model is being investigated by the Advertising Standards Authority.

Explanation of intro

> The woman has a silver watch wrapped round her upper arm, with the slogan: 'Put some weight on.'

> 'We're investigating it on the grounds that it might be distressing and upsetting to people with eating disorders,' said a spokesman for the authority. It had received 78 complaints from people with anorexia or bulimia, from relatives and friends of sufferers, and from the Eating Disorder Association.

Further information and quotes

> An Accurist spokesman said the company had also received complaints, and claimed that the advertisement was no longer running. 'There was never any intention to cause distress,' he said. Models One, the agency used by Zoya, the model in question, said that she was naturally thin and 'an exceptionally beautiful girl'.
> *Guardian*

Quotes from the people and organisations involved in stories are an essential part of their development. The story above, having quoted the Advertising Standards Authority, includes comments from the company and model agency. Readers – except the most bigoted – want to be given both sides of a story.

Conflicts between people and organisations – in politics, business, court cases – often make news. If the issue is complicated, the intro should be an attempt to simplify it without distortion. As the story is developed it will become easier to deal with the complications.

In the story below the reporter (or sub) has decided to lead on the technical victory won by McDonald's and not overload the intro by including the fact that two of the claims made by the Green campaigners were found to be justified. But this fact must be included early in the story.

Intro

> McDonald's won a hollow victory over two Green campaigners yesterday after the longest libel trial in history.

First retelling of intro

The hamburger corporation was awarded £60,000 damages over a leaflet which savaged its reputation, accusing it of putting profits before people, animal welfare and rain forests.

But the verdict cost more than £10 million in legal bills, which McDonald's will never recover from the penniless protesters who fought for three years in the High Court.

New fact

David Morris and Helen Steel were also claiming victory last night after the judge backed two of their claims. In an 800-page judgment which took six months to prepare, Mr Justice Bell ruled that the company is cruel to animals and that its advertising takes advantage of susceptible young children.

First retelling of intro (continued)

Mr Morris, 43, and 31-year-old Miss Steel are refusing to pay a penny of the damages. 'They don't deserve any money,' said Miss Steel, a part-time barmaid. 'And in any case, we haven't got any.'

Further information – background

The trial began in June 1994 and spanned 314 days in court, involving 180 witnesses and 40,000 pages of documents.

At its heart was the leaflet What's Wrong with McDonald's?, produced by the tiny pressure group London Greenpeace, which is not connected to Greenpeace International. The defendants helped to distribute it in the 1980s.

McDonald's had issued similar libel writs many times before, and opponents had always backed down. But Mr Morris and Miss Steel, vegetarian anarchists from Tottenham, North London, were determined to fight.

The burger firm hired one of the most brilliant legal teams money can buy, headed by Richard Rampton QC. The defendants were forced to represent themselves because there is no legal aid for libel cases. Former postman Mr Morris, a single parent with an eight-year-old son, appeared in court in casual dress, usually unshaven. Miss Steel, the daughter of a retired company director from Farnham, Surrey, prepared for the case each morning while hanging from a strap on the Piccadilly Line tube.

Second retelling of intro

Yesterday Mr Justice Bell ruled that they had libelled McDonald's by alleging that the corporation ripped down rain forests, contributed to Third World starvation, created excessive waste and sold food which was closely linked with heart disease and cancer.

He said it was also libellous to claim that McDonald's was interested in recruiting only cheap labour and exploited disadvantaged groups, particularly women and black people, although the claim was 'partly justified' because the firm pays low wages.

Further information and quotes

The judge also condemned as 'most unfair' the practice of sending young staff home early if the restaurant was quiet and not paying them for the rest of their shift.

Critics of the company will also seize on his ruling that McDonald's 'are culpably responsible for cruel practices in the rearing and slaughter of some of the animals which are used to produce their food'.

After the hearing, McDonald's UK president Paul Preston said he had no wish to bankrupt Mr Morris and Miss Steel. 'This was not a matter of costs, it was a matter of truth,' he said.

But the case has been a public relations disaster for McDonald's, cast in the role of a hugely rich corporation using its financial muscle to suppress debate on important issues. Far from the leaflet being suppressed, two million copies have now been handed out around the world.
Daily Mail

2 Splitting the pyramid

The pyramid structure is far easier to sustain if the intro is single rather than double. One of the problems with A + B intros is that they are difficult to develop coherently. The double intro below illustrates the problem:

Intro (A)

Bill Clinton has completed his selection of the most diverse Cabinet in US history by appointing the country's first woman law chief.

Intro (B)

The President-elect also picked a fourth black and a second Hispanic to join his top team.

Retelling of intro A

Zoe Baird, currently general counsel for the insurance company Aetna Life & Casualty, will be his Attorney General.

Retelling of intro B

Black representative Mike Espy was named Mr Clinton's secretary for agriculture while former mayor of Denver Federico Pena, a Hispanic, will be responsible for transport issues.
Daily Mail

Another strategy for the double intro is to develop part A before returning to part B:

Intro (A + B)

Australian Lucas Parsons equalled the course record with a nine-under-par 64, but still could not quite take the spotlight away from Tiger Woods in the first round of the Australian Masters in Melbourne yesterday.

Retelling of intro A

Parsons fired six birdies on the front nine before holing his second shot at the par four 13th for an eagle two – the highlight of the round. His approach shot landed on the green and bounced two metres beyond the flag, but then spun back into the hole.

Parsons now shares the Huntingdale course record with compatriot Mike Clayton and German Bernhard Langer.

Quotes supporting intro A

'My game has been getting better over recent months. This is a course I know and I can play well here,' said Parsons. 'I got off to a good start today and it just kept happening. I just went with the flow.'

Retelling of intro B

But Woods, who won the Bangkok Classic in Thailand on Sunday, his fourth tournament victory since turning professional last August, was still the centre of attention.

Development of B and quotes

He also enjoyed the long holes to finish at five-under-par 68 for a share of fifth place to remain in contention.

The 21-year-old big-hitting American birdied all four par fives on the par-73 course to the delight of a large gallery, even though he only used his driver once.

'I grinded my way around there and came in with a good score. Off the tee, it was probably one of my better ball-striking rounds in a while,' Woods said.

'It was just the mental grind of playing a golf course that requires accuracy and so much precision off the tee. You don't really have a chance to relax.

'I haven't played my best golf today. I just made one birdie besides the par fives and that's not saying a whole lot.'

Further information

Australian Peter O'Malley held second place with a 65. Former US Masters champion Larry Mize finished on five-under alongside Woods, while defending champion Craig Parry, of Australia, struggled to a 73.
Daily Telegraph

Splitting the pyramid always presents problems. Either, as in the first example above, you make the reader hop about from A to B as the story unfolds – now it's A, now it's B. Or, as in the second example, you develop A fully before turning to B. The problem here is that B can get forgotten before the reader reaches it.

It cannot be stressed too strongly that the best intro is always the simplest: try to find one point for your intro rather than two – or more. In terms of development this may mean (as in the *Daily Mail* story on McDonald's above) that you need to introduce important material not covered by the intro early in the story. But that is a better solution than cluttering the intro and confusing the general development of the story.

3 Exceptions to the pyramid

Don't worship the pyramid: it is only a way of visualising the most common structure of a traditional news story. The guiding principle in developing a news story is: what does the reader need or want to know

now? If answering their questions means abandoning the pyramid, go ahead.

Speech reports, for example, are not necessarily written in strict pyramid form. They should start with the most important point made by the speaker – but this will often be followed by other points that have little to do with the first. Of course, you should try to put these secondary points in order of importance but this may seem a pretty arbitrary process.

However, to keep the pyramid idea, each point can be seen as a mini-pyramid with its own intro, development and elaborating quote; thus the story can become a series of small pyramids.

4 The narrative style

The clearest example of non-pyramid news writing is a story in the narrative style, which begins with a dramatic moment and carries on to the end – often the point of the story. If you cut a narrative news story from the end you destroy it.

The one concession made to conventional news writing is that the main character is often asked for a quote, which is added on after the narrative ending.

Intro

> When Bernard Warner examined the lobster it did not strike him as being particularly odd. The crustacean looked paler than its rivals but it had arrived at Mr Warner's fishmonger shop in Doncaster as part of a routine delivery from the East coast, so there could not be anything unusual about it, could there?

Story continues

> Deciding the animal was simply suffering from old age, Mr Warner flew to Madeira on holiday. En route, his in-flight magazine fell open at an article about albino lobsters.
>
> A white lobster caught off the American coast was sold for £15,000, the article told him. A bigger version caught off Filey was insured for £20,000.

Story ends

> Mr Warner raced to a phone after touching down. 'Don't sell that lobster,' he breathlessly told his family firm. It was too late. The

creature – worth £20,000 – had been sold on at the normal market rate, boiled and digested by an unsuspecting diner somewhere.

Quote

Mr Warner, who has been in the fish business for 40 years, sells his lobsters to restaurants and private customers throughout the country, and he has no idea where his prize catch went.

He said: 'I couldn't believe it. In all my time as a fishmonger I've never come across one before. I'm pig sick.'

'Someone has had a very valuable meal without even knowing it. For me it's like winning the lottery and then discovering you have thrown the ticket away.'
Guardian

NEWS STYLE

News style is – or ought to be – plain, simple, clear, so that the story tells itself. For a detailed discussion of this issue, see the final chapter.

Variation

One of the worst news-writing habits you can acquire is to avoid calling a spade a spade – or rather, having called it a spade in the intro, to insist on calling it a gardening tool, a digging device and then a horticultural implement in the pars that follow.

This practice is based on two false assumptions: one, that the repetition of words like spade is always a bad idea; two, that attentive readers enjoy these variation words for their own sake.

Precisely the opposite is true – as is shown by the story above. A lively tale about a special kind of lobster is weakened by the inept use of a series of variation words to refer to it: 'crustacean' in par one; 'animal' in par two; 'creature' in par four.

These words add nothing: they are clearly examples of variation for its own sake. And if the reader has half an ear they grate. 'Crustacean' is particularly naff: it echoes those old football reports where 'the 35-year-old goalkeeper Wally Jones' becomes 'the veteran net-minder' in the next par.

By contrast the reporter just gets away with 'prize catch' in par five – though it would have been better if Mr Warner had done the catching in the first place. But it was a prize; it had been caught; and the phrase adds the right kind of emphasis.

Some 10 years after the lobster story quoted above the *Guardian* published a news feature about the increasing popularity of the shellfish best known as 'langoustines' (that's the French word – they're also known by their Italian name 'scampi' and as Dublin Bay prawns and Norway lobsters). According to the gourmet's bible, *Larousse Gastronomique*, 'This marine crustacean of the lobster family resembles a freshwater crayfish' – not, you'll notice, a prawn. But in the *Guardian* piece the words 'langoustine' and 'prawn' are used interchangeably. The picture caption, for example, reads:

> Frank Ronald . . . sorts a day's catch of langoustine after returning to Loch Fyne, Argyll. The prawn is about to hit the mass market . . .

This kind of variation has traditionally been called 'elegant' – because it's intended to embellish, to add colour to copy. But it rarely adds anything – except confusion.

Then there is variation to avoid unintended repetition. Your ear should tell you when this is necessary. But remember that the plainer the word the less noticeable it is when repeated, so don't bother to avoid repeating words like 'said' and 'says'.

Sometimes repetition tells you that the sentence itself is badly constructed – too long, too loose, too complicated. Here's an example with the repeated word in italic type:

> A mother of three young *children*, jailed for two months after lying about a traffic accident, was yesterday reunited with her *children* after she was freed by three Appeal Court judges – but they reiterated the gravity of the offence and said the plight of her *children* had tipped the balance in favour of her release.
> *Guardian*

About the only thing to be said in favour of this intro is that 'children' does not become 'offspring' in the second case and 'progeny' or 'issue' in the third. If you find yourself writing a sentence like this, don't struggle to replace the repeated words: rewrite the sentence altogether in a simpler way.

Quotes

First, in general, use 'said'/'says' to introduce and attribute quotes, though 'told'/'tells' is a useful variation, as in 'the minister told MPs'. So do not write:

> Speaking at the meeting the speaker said . . .

but:

> The speaker told the meeting . . .

Always avoid variations like 'claim', 'admit', 'state', 'remark', 'point out', 'explain', 'refute' – unless you intend the precise meaning conveyed by the word.

Do not use 'he added' because you think the quote has been going on long enough and are too lazy to think up some other way of getting to the next bit. Keep 'he added' for cases where there is a pause, an afterthought or a contrast as in:

> He said it would probably rain – but he added: 'We need it.'

Where possible use the present tense – 'says' – instead of the past – 'said'. When somebody is quoted for the first time put the attribution at the beginning, as in:

> John Smith says: 'I'm furious.'

If the attribution does not come at the beginning, put it after the first complete sentence – not in the middle of it and not at the end of the complete quote. This is the way to do it:

> 'I'm furious,' John Smith says. 'I've never been so angry.'

Consistency

Be consistent. Don't change your tone in the middle of a story. Either write in the traditional style or use one of the variations; be serious or light – not both at the same time.

Particularly avoid the facetious remark dropped into a straightforward story. As the columnist Keith Waterhouse once put it:

The interpolation of a weak joke into a serious news story is so inappropriate that it can only be described as oafish.

Bridges and links

In general news does not need bridges to connect one par with the next. Transitional words and phrases like 'also' – or the pompous equivalent 'in addition' – are rarely necessary. When you start a new sentence or a new par you are effectively saying to the reader: 'also'. That does not mean that these words and phrases are always wrong but you should not strain to include them in traditional news stories.

Journalese and jargon

Most of what is called journalese – whether downmarket ('axe' for 'sack') or upmarket ('sustain injury' for 'be hurt') – is bad writing and you should avoid it. 'Following' for 'after' is certainly an example of this.

But certain code words can be useful – to maximise the amount of information you can convey to the reader. For example, if you're pretty confident – but not certain – that A will happen, you can write: 'A is set to happen.' You should always try to find out precisely what somebody's role is in something – but if you can't, it's usually better to write 'B is involved with the project' rather than nothing at all.

The same advice covers phrases like 'industry sources say' when your contacts will not give you identified quotes. Inform your reader – but keep the jargon under control.

Names and titles

The convention in journalism is full name ('John/Joan Smith') for the first use, then either courtesy title ('Mr/Mrs/Miss/Ms Smith) or surname or first name for the rest of the story. (For more on this and similar points see the chapter on house style in *Subediting for Journalists*.) Remember, be consistent: never follow 'John Smith' by 'Mr Smith', then 'John'. Again, variation for its own sake irritates the reader.

Endings

In general, traditional news stories (as opposed to those in the narrative style) do not have endings – that is, they end where the writer runs out of steam, the sub runs out of space, the reader runs out of interest. But there is no reason why a news story should not end neatly. The exception proves that the rule is one of pragmatism not principle:

> BT is tightening up its telephone security system after its confidential list of ex-directory numbers was penetrated – by a woman from Ruislip.
>
> Working from home, Rachel Barry, a middle-aged married mother, conned BT into revealing the ex-directory numbers of celebrities, sports stars and people in the news . . .
>
> Last week Mrs Barry was convicted by Harrow magistrates of 12 offences of obtaining personal data and selling it to national newspapers . . .
>
> It is believed Mrs Barry had been operating the scam for several years and had earned thousands of pounds. She pleaded guilty to all 12 offences and was fined a total of £1,200 and ordered to pay costs of £800.
>
> Last night the *Observer* was unable to contact Mrs Barry by telephone. She is ex directory.
> *Observer*

That is an ending.

TWO NEWS STORIES

MAN KILLED AS L-DRIVE CAR PLUNGES OFF CLIFF

A man was feared dead last night after his car ran off a 150ft clifftop into rough seas when his girlfriend lost control while he was giving her a driving lesson.

The woman, in her early 20s, scrambled from the Ford Fiesta as it crashed through a low stone wall at the edge of a car park at the Beacon, St Agnes, on the north Cornwall coast.

Andrew Dunklin, 25, from St Agnes, was trapped in the vehicle as it rolled over the cliff. It is thought he was thrown through the windscreen into the sea. The car came to rest in 30ft of water and immediately began to break up.

The woman raised the alarm and coastguards launched a rescue operation which at its height involved a Navy helicopter, divers, two lifeboats and a cliff rescue team.

Insp Paul Whetter of Devon & Cornwall police said the woman had managed to get out just before the car went over the cliff.

She was treated for shock at the scene by paramedics before being taken to Treliske Hospital in Truro.

A neighbour looking after the missing man's mother at her home in the village said: 'She has just lost her only son.'

The search operation was hampered by worsening weather and a Navy diver had to be pulled out of the sea. The St Agnes and St Ives inshore lifeboats could not get close to the spot.

'We sent our cliff man down to a point about 60ft above the waves, where the cliff became a sheer drop,' said Mike North, sector manager with HM Coastguard. 'He was able to keep an eye on the scene and spotted a lot of debris from the car.

'He saw some clothing and the inshore lifeboat was able to pick up the girl's bag floating in the water.'

A spokesman for RNAS Culdrose added: 'The first diver in the water said it was too dangerous for others to go in. He was being pounded by pieces of wreckage from the car which was being smashed on to the rocks at the bottom of the cliffs.'

The search was called off at 5pm because the situation had become 'too dangerous' for rescue workers. It was to be resumed at first light today.

Mr Dunklin is understood to have been giving his girlfriend a driving lesson on Beacon Road, a remote and little-used track near the cliffs. They may have driven into the gravel-surfaced car park to practise reversing or three-point turns.
Daily Telegraph

This is a stark and terrible story simply told. The reporter has no need to strain for effect here.

The intro is a bit long at 31 words – a tabloid would have shortened 'when his girlfriend lost control while he was giving her a driving lesson' to something like 'when a driving lesson went wrong'. But because the words and clauses are straightforward, the intro works well enough.

Then, because the intro tells so much of the story, the second par can add dramatic detail as well as locating the story. But do we really want to know what make of car it was? Well, yes, the ordinariness of the Ford Fiesta helps to make this a story about any young couple.

The third par retells the intro; the fourth introduces the rescue operation; but rather than turn the story sideways to cover the search, the reporter rightly concentrates on the two people involved in the accident – and the man's mother.

When we get to it, halfway through the story, the search is described with the aid of powerful quotes. Finally, there's a par on how the couple came to be at the clifftop.

A few quibbles: 'vehicle' in the third par is unnecessary variation for 'car': it follows 'Ford Fiesta'; RNAS (towards the end) should be given in full; in the same par 'added' is particularly strange, suggesting that the two people quoted were in the same room – and the woman would surely be named if police had released her name.

But in general the reporter has made good use of an opportunity to let a strong story tell itself without clutter and melodramatic language.

HOBBIES PUT JUDGE ON THE ROAD TO RUIN

A judge's entry in *Who's Who* listed his passions as cars and drinking with friends. Yesterday these twin interests landed John Aspinall QC in court, where he was banned from the road for two and a half years for drink-driving.

Aspinall, 50, who worked as a lorry driver before becoming a lawyer, was more than three times over the limit when he caused a crash on Good Friday.

In *Who's Who* he lists his recreations as 'motor sports' and 'being with my wife and friends at the Drax Arms' – the country pub near his home in Spetisbury, Dorest, where he is a popular regular.

Now his career is in tatters. He has resigned as a crown court recorder, a part-time judge, and faces a Bar Council disciplinary hearing which could mean being suspended from practising as a barrister or even thrown out of the profession.

He has also resigned from the judicial committee of the governing body of the RAC motorsports council.

Magistrates at Blandford in Dorset were told Aspinall had a blood alcohol level of 122mg. The legal limit is 35mg. He admitted drink-driving and was fined £1,800 and told his ban could be cut by six months if he takes a driver-rehabilitation course.

Daily Mail

A routine 'judge banned for drink-driving' court report has been turned into a lively story because somebody has bothered to check Aspinall's entry in *Who's Who*.

The all-important intro is a form of delayed drop: the first sentence sets up the second. Then after some basic information on the offence, the sequence is repeated: quotes from *Who's Who* are followed by more on Aspinall's ruined career.

Only in the last par do we get the details of the offence and the magistrates' decision. This must appear somewhere in the story – but only as a tailpiece.

There are blemishes: 'twin interests' in the second sentence is a curious variation on 'passions' in the first; and there is a clumsy phrase in the fourth par, 'which could mean being suspended'.

But, as a whole, the story is an example of modern news writing, which grabs the reader's attention, then keeps it by answering their questions.

3
Writing features
Sally Adams

The joy of feature writing lies in its variety. Anything from a celebrity interview to an agony column, a product round-up to an obit, can be considered a feature and this variety demands versatility. If there's one word that describes good feature writers it's savvy.

The sole constraint for features is to write in the way that's right for the publication, its editor and its readers. What suits *Car* won't necessarily do for *Custom Car*. What suits *Shoot* is unlikely to work for *Four Four Two* or *When Saturday Comes*. Being so varied, features are hard to define. The safest guide is negative: they're not news.

Not being news, they're liberated from spare, functional prose. In place of the breathless messenger they can be entertaining gossips, perceptive analysts, eccentric experts, sympathetic counsellors, bitchy snoops, inspiring guides.

Because they're so varied they're harder to write. They build on everything learnt as a news reporter and in addition demand that writers attract and hold the reader's attention without the benefit of a narrative pull. They can require that writers research and master complicated subjects, then reduce huge chunks of information into accessible, digestible copy. Reporters rarely mutate effortlessly into feature writers. The apprenticeship varies from months to years.

Unlike news reporters, who work within pre-agreed formulas, feature writers don't need immutable structures. Ask five journalists to cover a car crash and they'd almost certainly deliver recognisably similar copy acceptable to a number of newspapers. Ask five journalists to write a feature on car crashes and, first, you'd be asked for what publication. Then you'd receive five very different features, each aimed at a selected audience. Feature writing requires a different way of thinking, writing and structuring. Feature writers are free to take risks; they're the sky divers of print journalism.

GUIDELINES

Though feature writers are not burdened by lengthy rules, there are many guidelines they should heed, plus a few imperatives. These are ignored at the writer's peril. The most important are:

- Know who you're writing for, their interests and concerns. (Otherwise how can you gain and retain their attention?)
- Know what you want to say and achieve. (Take time to write a brief. It pays rich dividends.)
- Think, think, think – and go on thinking. (Feature writers are valued for the freshness of their approach.)

Effective feature writing is accessible, interesting, lively, colourful, grabbing and relevant. For writers to achieve these results depends, first, on accepting a simple principle: that the communicator takes total responsibility for getting the message across.

In ascending order of difficulty, features can inform, help, amuse, persuade and inspire to action. Gradations exist within all these categories. The difficulty in writing to 'inform', for example, ranges from providing coherent and accessible data to offering analysis and promoting understanding. 'Persuade' ranges in difficulty from prompting a reader to try a new hairstyle to convincing them to try a new lifestyle.

A study of what editors and feature editors look for, conducted over many years, produced remarkably similar answers. The highest common factors were that features should:

- involve the reader
- be accurate
- be readable
- have a grabbing intro
- meet the brief
- have substance
- be well crafted
- contain . . . (the X factor: an added element of surprise on a subject specific to the publication).

RATING IMPACT

When editors and feature editors receive fresh copy they don't reach for a tick-box list to check requirements have been met. Instead, knowingly or not, they read the feature to discover the answers to certain vital questions. These have been borrowed from a former chairman of the Man Booker Prize panel, who asked himself four questions when assessing books – questions that work remarkably well for features.

> Personally, I found myself asking four questions . . . Could I read it? If I could read it, did I believe it? If I believed it, did I care about it? If I cared, what was the quality of my caring, and would it last?
> Few, very few, survived as far as question four. Far too many relied on the classic formula of a beginning, a muddle and an end.
> Philip Larkin

Applying these questions to a feature means asking:

1   Did I read it to the end? Was it smoothly written, taking me effortlessly from A to Z?
2   If I read to the end, was I convinced by what I read? Was it accurate and authoritative?
3   If I was convinced, did I care? Was it relevant? Did I feel involved?
4   If I care, am I going to do anything about it? Cut out and keep the feature? Show it to friends? Follow the expert advice? Learn from that example? Put those suggestions into operation? Write to the editor?

Editors are delighted with features that reach Stage 4. The many ways that writers make that happen are the substance of page 52 onwards.

A QUICK WORD BEFORE YOU START

The quality of the questions you ask yourself before you start writing is crucial. The sharper your questions, the more likely you are to produce stylish copy. Best advice is to spend a considerable time thinking about fresh ways to approach the subject as early as possible. That's most likely to produce lively, appealing and original copy.

Readers approach features very much as they approach food. Some want plain fare, some fancy cooking, some heavy stodge. Very few relish stale cheese sandwiches or froth. To labour the simile, good ingredients and preparation are essential.

As always, writing for the readers is the key. This doesn't mean playing safe and giving them more of what they liked last time. Slavishly following market research has been the death of many a publication. Offer readers an amalgam of known success with a dash of surprise. 'I want to see five new facts in every feature,' demanded the first, highly successful editor of *Marie Claire*.

Before even thinking about feature ideas, wise writers and editors make certain that they and their writers know the publication's editorial policy. If you don't know what you're trying to achieve, you're dangerously directionless. Unlike mission statements, editorial policies are neither pious nor pretentious. They're practical and generally start in the infinitive and list three or four of the publication's most important tasks.

Common examples include: to inform, to help, to improve, to unite, to enthuse, to persuade, to entertain, to inspire . . . Clearly, the words chosen 'to inform' will be different from those chosen 'to persuade', requiring differing approaches and vocabulary.

The next component describes the readers. Not all these factors need to be considered for every feature but getting to know the readers is essential:

- circulation (how many buy/subscribe to the publication or receive free copies)
- readership (how many read the publication)
- average age range
- male/female split
- years of education – this affects words used and sentence complexity
- interests
- job title for b2b
- disposable income of consumer publications (general public) or budget available (b2b)
- where readers live
- political/religious/social persuasions
- what makes them happy
- their greatest anxieties
- if known, how long they spend reading the publication.

The last, and optional, component, is a target. For example, for a weekly: 'Every issue we'll scoop the opposition with at least two features about people in the news'; 'We'll persuade more readers to enter the photography competition'; 'We'll win the local paper of the year contest.'

The same . . . but different

Whatever type of publication a journalist writes for – newspaper, consumer magazine, b2b magazine or newsletter – the basic approach is the same: write for your readers.

Journalists writing for newspapers and consumer magazines usually know more about their subjects than most of their readers, so their main task is to capture the reader's interest. However, with b2b magazines the readers themselves are specialists who often know more about the business than the writer does. This presents the journalist with different challenges but also rewards. With the thousands of b2b magazines published in the UK there is obviously a market for feature writers prepared to specialise.

FEATURE PROCESS

Once the necessary foundations are soundly laid, the creative feature process proper can begin. For the most complex articles it runs this way: Idea, Brief, Research, Interviewing, Plan, Write. For simpler, say first-person, features it's possible to go straight from Brief to Plan, as the writer has lived the research and has no need to interview him/herself.

Features start from an *idea*, which should suit the publication and interest the readership. There are few, if any, that are new. Two initial factors to consider are time and manageability. It's best to avoid features needing quotes from European academics in August, for example, because of the great escape from the heat of the cities. Similarly, avoid needing phone interviews with Singapore businessmen for a UK publication because of the time difference, unless you are able to work very early in the morning or late at night.

Ideas like 'Music in the movies' or 'Miscarriages of justice' aren't features, they're books. It's essential to slice them into manageable proportions, looking at trends in three recent British movie scores, for example, or examining four current justice campaigns. The more frequent the publication, the thinner the slice. Salami for dailies, thick toast for monthlies.

The *brief* is where many beginners go wrong, mostly because they consider it a waste of time. Far from it: a well-thought-out brief provides direction and shape. Ideally it should include:

- deadline
- length
- the angle/approach you are adopting
- the tone (campaigning/informative/entertaining . . .)
- the scope/limits of the feature – what you plan to include/omit
- what's wanted: colourful quotes; background info; detailed facts; analysis . . .
- questions you want answered
- questions the editor wants answered
- where to go for research
- any extras: boxes, stat tables, pictures, illustrations.

Beware the editor/features editor who refuses to brief, saying airily 'You know what I want.' Experience shows this often involves a complex subject not thought through carefully enough. Editors may have a fuzzy notion of what they think they want but they know exactly what they *don't* want when they see it. If you are not given a brief, you should work one out, then go back and agree it with them.

A brief provides the basic structure and eases you into the next stage: *research*. Be warned. There's a lot of horrendous and dangerously inaccurate info on the web. Use but don't necessarily rely on Google. If you are interested in what appears to be a relevant report, quote or interview, then check the original source and *date* very carefully. The info could be years old and could land you and the publication in serious difficulty. Corroborate any stats that could be dodgy, double check when possible and never – well, hardly ever – trust spelling on the web, even on some of the home pages.

Original research (look at books?) and interviews often provide the bonus that editors prize: fresh facts, lively and unexpected quotes, copy that elicits the 'never-knew-that' reaction. Don't rush here. Capsule advice is: start early, think laterally, go to a reliable source and note sources. Stick with research. Make that extra phone call. Dig for that extra hour.

Interviewing comes next. Think, analyse, plan and focus as before and don't model your approach on John Humphrys or Jeremy Paxman. Don't start until you know what you want to know. If you're interviewing someone experienced at dealing with the press, try to make it interesting for them too, and remember they're well used to the wiles of journalists. Never ask celebrities the first question that springs to mind; it's likely to have sprung to every other mind as well. Celebrities apart, always ask the obvious as well as stimulating questions. With most feature subjects, the skill is to get them to drop their defences and talk.

Go in/pick up the phone only when you're thoroughly prepared and know exactly what you want to know. Don't talk too much but listen intently and intelligently to what's said and, finally, trade places and consider the impact of your questions. You won't get a good interview with a research scientist who uses vivisection if you start: 'How can you possibly be involved in such a contemptible business?'

Be sceptical not adversarial. Hostile questions elicit good quotes but it's best to start nice and turn nasty later. Interviewers would do well to keep the American saying in mind: 'You get more flies with honey than vinegar.' And never, ever, forget that they are the star, and are not there simply to provide you with required facts or opinions.

Once you've completed the research and interviewing, pause. It's too soon to start writing. *Plan* your structure. You don't have to follow it slavishly, but forethought pays proven dividends in saving time and angst.

Logically, the next section should be about structure but, as most graduate-entry writers learn, journalism has little to do with logic. It's easier to break features down into their component parts, analyse them and then go on to assembling a sweet-running whole rather than plunge straight into the most complex part of the writer's craft.

One final, cynical observation: anyone who works for an editor they rate as an idiot will have to please that idiot if they want to see their work in print. Tough, but if it's your first job, you should consider that you might be wrong. It's amazing how much most editors know.

NEED-TO-DECIDE FACTORS

Publication? Are you writing for a broadsheet (also called quality/ serious since no longer broad-sized), tabloid or redtop newspaper, a consumer magazine, customer magazine, business magazine, technical, trade or specialist magazine or newsletter?

Readers? Do you know the publication's editorial policy? Do you know as much as possible about the readers (see page 48)?

Content and approach? How many words are wanted? Vast choice from 8,000 (*Vanity Fair*), down to 'featurettes' at 300–350. Best to deliver *slightly* more than required as it's easier to cut than fill.

Deadline? Try to be realistic.

Genre/type? Will the feature be news-pegged (inspired by or linked to a news story), investigative, a think piece (your views on a given subject), analysis (subject assessed with pro and con quotes and facts), a personalised column?

Subject/angle? Huge choice again: celebrities are astonishingly popular as subjects, with angles being almost anything – celebrity profile, celebrity gossip, fashion, heartbreak, new house, new dog – there seems no end; business ditto, individuals or groups (sports teams, orchestras, clubs, councils); specialist topics (fashion, cooking, motoring, travel, history, jobs, children), product stories/reviews/tests?

Approach/tone? Will the feature be informative, helpful, inspiring, campaigning, funny, critical?

Style? What's wanted? Lots of quotes, anecdotes, facts, info from cuttings, research, 'colour' (copy focusing on description or impression, subjective approach)?

Display/appearance? Solid text or separated sections, case histories?

Extras? Stats, tables, boxes, pull quotes, summaries?

INTROS

The following sample intros are likely to provoke mixed reactions. They cannot please everyone – that's a given. But if your first reaction is to dismiss any of them out of hand, you should ask yourself whether you are responding as yourself rather than as a reader of the particular publication.

> '*It's no good standing there at the beginning of an article flexing your muscles. Just do the old handspring right away.*'
> 'Cassandra', Mirror

The subs and the editor are paid to read what you write; readers you have to grab. Most glance first at the headline, illustrations, maybe the stand-first (short informative display copy giving clearer idea of the feature's content). Only then do they read the intro. You have 10 seconds max in which to catch them.

> *Sesame Street* lied. America's not full of black and white kids, all learning together in multi-racial harmony. Down in LA, Big Bird's toting an AK and the Cookie Monster's doing crack.
> Big Issue

The power of this intro lies in its opening sentence, with the strong and unexpected verb 'lied'. '*Sesame Street* has been lying' wouldn't work as well.

The powerful start is followed with rich examples that conjure up funny, dramatic pictures. The rhythm of the last sentence works because it's in the right order, nailed down at the end by the single syllable 'crack'. It would be less effective if the Cookie Monster preceded Big Bird. If you doubt this, read the transposed sentence aloud.

> The groom fell asleep in his mother's lap. The bride burst into tears and had to be silenced with a piece of fruit. Dhanraj was four, his bride Santosh was seven. The wedding, which would change their lives forever, meant nothing to them. It was their parents who recited the marriage vows, their parents who circled the sacred fire seven times on their small and sleepy children's behalf.
> Rosalyn Chissick, Elle

Here's another example of surprising juxtaposition: childhood and marriage. All the words are carefully chosen. 'Recited' has greater ceremonial overtones than 'repeated'. 'Silenced' rather than 'comforted' shows that something important is happening. The 'sacred fire' and 'seven' import mystic hints about a solemn ceremony, contrasting with the touching 'small and sleepy children'.

There's no one way to write an intro, only the way that's right for the feature and the publication. The approach you select should spring from what you judge will most interest your readers. Content and style both have their part to play. The test of a good intro is that it grabs and keeps readers' attention, making them want to read on.

Intros to avoid are those which bemuse, bore and activate the switch-off factor. So swap heads with the readers and avoid anything they could consider trite, banal, convoluted, negative, patronising or irrelevant and don't include too many sets of initials, abbreviations or acronyms. Worst of all, don't write anything that can be dismissed with a weary 'So what?'

Types of intro

These five categories are useful as guides; in practice, many excellent intros combine two or more elements.

Strong/provocative/intriguing statement
Narrative/anecdote
Description/scene-setting
Question that buttonholes the reader
Quote

1 Statement

The most common way to start a feature, capable of almost infinite variation. Usually relies for impact on contrast, colour and surprise.

> We British still lead the world in something. Unfortunately, it's tabloid journalism.
> Adam Sweeting, *Guardian*

A straightforward, hard-to-resist first sentence. Opinionated second sentence, spot-on for *Guardian* readers. It's a variation of the 'build 'em up, knock 'em down' approach, with the punch words at the end.

> Sir Alex Ferguson's secret dressing-room doctrine – cornerstone of his sustained success at Manchester United – can finally be revealed to the outside world.
> David McDonnell, *Mirror*

Irresistible – even to those who don't play football, don't follow football, don't care about football at all. To prove this thesis, here's the dressing-room doctrine revealed again. If you don't read on, you're a very rare person indeed.

> The SIX most important words: 'I ADMIT I MADE A MISTAKE'.
>
> The FIVE most important words: 'YOU DID A GOOD JOB'.
>
> The FOUR most important words: 'WHAT IS YOUR OPINION?'
>
> The THREE most important words: 'IF YOU PLEASE'.
>
> The TWO most important words: 'THANK YOU'.
>
> The ONE most important word: 'WE'.
>
> The LEAST important word: 'I'.

Now you know. It's understandably preachy and just a tad disappointing that it's so simple but – wow – it has worked magnificently.

> Lauren Bacall is not a legend. Not yet, anyway. 'If I'm a legend, I'm dead,' she says. 'Do you want me to be dead? Legends are of the past.' This is typical Bacall: 82 years old she may be, but she remains as bold, bullish and brassy as the day she first sauntered onto the screen more than 60 years ago. The woman once dubbed The Look now just shoots them with those steely grey eyes of hers. 'I have no respect for celebrities,' she continues, 'and I object to being called one, so don't try it! I'm an actress, not a celebrity.'
> James Mottram, *Independent*

The short, sharp, surprising first sentence is suddenly put into perspective by an even shorter, sharper second sentence. The next two are just as condensed. All define the Bacall territory. In just 29 words Bacall's character has been vividly established.

Words quick-march on. Her age is revealed, then her personality captured in three cunningly chosen adjectives which have a rhythm approaching a chant: bold, bullish and brassy . . . bold, bullish and brassy. So the par continues, slowing down with 'sauntered', then speeding up again for the summary, another broadside from Bacall making it clear exactly how she wants to be treated. 'I'm an actress, not a celebrity.' By quoting this, Mottram in effect says: 'This is Lauren Bacall. I'm going to play by her rules because I know this way she'll talk.' Which she did.

> I hate kids. Hate them all without exception. Even yours. Especially yours. Especially if it's a boy and you named it Jake. And if you've

> ever written a chummy diary article about Jake for a Sunday sup-
> plement, I wish nothing short of death upon you. Death by wasps
> and bombs and razorwire. In a thunderstorm. While Jake looks on
> in horror. Because I hate parents too.
> Charlie Brooker, *Guardian*

A machinegun-like attack, provocative by design, super-opinionated, meant to infuriate and entertain. He only does it to annoy because he knows . . . well, he knows it will prompt lots of emails, letters and phone calls to the editor, which is one certain way of upping your value (see 'Rating impact', page 47). Brooker makes a living from scoffing, attacking, belittling, questioning but also (occasionally) from saluting, praising and approving, all in ways that involve readers. Not easy.

Memo to would-be columnists: before you start, check pages 78–80.

> A statue in his honour, a guest slot in *The Simpsons* and more
> appearances in the *Daily Mirror* than David Beckham. Not bad for
> a man who's never done a stroke of work in his life. It's Mr Andy
> Capp.
> Jeremy Armstrong, *Mirror*

An intro that's a worthy member of the delayed-drop family (see page 27). At first – no doubt – it's about a person. Who could that be? Someone who rated a statue . . . who featured in a world-famous TV cartoon . . . who has never worked . . . ? Then comes the 'Gotcha!' It's Andy Capp, the cartoon character. The writer skilfully catches the readers out in very much the same way that Andy Capp always escapes work. (The feature was to celebrate Andy's 50th birthday.)

Fashion gets more pages than ever now, with descriptive captions giving way to sharp, stylish writing.

> Finally, after several seasons lurking about at the edge of the party
> like a shy guest in the wrong dress, the 80s trend has taken off. Just
> when you thought it was safe to ditch the leggings, a herd of other
> dinosaur outfits from 20 years ago is congregating on the horizon,
> about to stampede. Prepare yourself for a renaissance of extended
> shoulders, outsized knitwear, masses of black, acres of cling and –
> crucially – the funny little pixie boot.
> Mimi Spencer, *YOU*

Sometimes one judiciously selected word is a sufficient hook.

> This week's deplorable idea comes from [name]
> *Times* diary

It's very hard not to read on to find out what the *Times* business diarist so reviled.

2 Narrative/anecdote

> The scene was Kitzbuhel, the programme *Grandstand*. The event was the Men's Downhill. A man referred to as 'Britain's sole representative' came plummeting down the Streif. 'He won't be looking for a first place today,' said David Vine, 'he'll be looking for experience.'
>
> At that very instant – not a bit later, but while David was actually saying it – Britain's sole representative was upside down and plummeting into the crowd at 60mph plus. Spectators were mown down as if by grape-shot. The air was full of snow, beanies, mittens, bits of wood. You had to be watching to get the full impact. It was a kind of perfection.
> Clive James, *Observer*

The first two matter-of-fact sentences set the scene and get the intro swinging along freely. The first hint of something out of the ordinary comes with 'A man referred to', which is taken up and echoed to great effect in the second paragraph. Consider, too, the use of the word 'plummeting'.

Is there any other word that would do as well? 'Plummet' comes from the French *plomb* meaning lead, and it gives the feeling of a headlong descent as the skier descends almost vertically. There's no other word that works as well. The well-placed quote follows, broken up with the attribution to the hapless David Vine so that the full weight of the sentence falls on the key word 'experience'.

The second paragraph begins plainly but after the first phrase, 'At that very instant', goes into 'freeze frame' or slow motion as the writer repeats what he said earlier but at greater length. This works because it mirrors what people involved in traffic accidents experience, using a device beloved of film-makers: that slowing down at moments of intensity.

Earlier the skier was allowed just the one action word 'plummeting'. Now he's shown pictorially at greater length and the rest of the description works so well because it uses specific words: snow, beanies (bobble ski hats), mittens, bits of wood. All chosen to give the feeling of fragmentation and chaos.

> Exactly one year ago today, I tried to kill myself. Fortunately (or
> unfortunately as I felt at the time), I am blessed with an iron con-
> stitution. At 3.20am, I woke up. Through some sick irony (who says
> the heavens don't have a sense of humour?), it was the same time,
> to the minute, that I had been waking for a year before I was finally
> diagnosed with clinical depression.
> Sally Brampton, *Daily Telegraph*

Dramatic but not dramatised start, followed straightaway by revealing
details. The use of brackets is frowned on by many writers but is acceptable here exactly because they emphasise that her thought relates to the
past. Then comes the strange coincidence of waking at the same time,
another wry aside, and the par ends with the reason for the whole story.
Straightforward writing, powerful and honest.

Journalist-describes-meeting-famous-interviewee is one of the most common ways to begin a celebrity feature. So common, in fact, that it can be
deadly boring, a real heart-sinker. It's partly a reaction to the growing
power of PRs who can determine times, limits and subjects that can be
covered. So make the interview lively for the reader and as interesting as
you can for the interviewee. The more famous the celebrity, the harder it
is for the interviewer. One approach: go for revealing observations.

> Jack Dee is assiduously polite to the girl who serves him a cap-
> puccino at his London club. He smiles, moves aside any clutter
> from the table and says 'thank-you' twice. When she leaves he
> comments on how good the service is. It is something he always
> notices. He has never forgotten his days as a waiter.
> *Daily Express* Saturday magazine

3 Description/scene-setting

> A big-boned young man with wild hair escaping in all directions
> from under his baseball cap crouches by a jungle river, so excited
> that he can barely breathe. 'This is it! This is the one . . . a species
> completely new to horticulture in Britain,' he gasps. For a few
> magnificent moments, at this key point in his quest to track down
> extraordinary plants in the Australian rainforest, Tom Hart Dyke
> looks like Indiana Jones finding the Holy Grail – provided, that is,
> you ignore the giant yellow-and-white daisy printed on his sweaty
> T-shirt.
> Sandy Mitchell, *Daily Telegraph*

Very visual. The first sentence evokes a colourful picture of a passionate
gardener at his moment of triumph and it does so in the present tense,

using only adjectives to draw the picture. The remaining description comes from selected nouns and active verbs. His hair is escaping, he crouches, he can barely breathe. The quote in the second sentence captures his excitement, followed by a very necessary explanation of why he is there, reinforcing the find with a touch of showbiz.

> Marco Pierre White, fat hands waving, pale brown eyes staring . . . has been awake all night, 20 hours in a solicitor's office discussing a 'huge deal' and you can smell his armpits a table away.
> Katharine Viner, *Guardian*

Sometimes a few colourful adjectives are necessary. Nice catering touch, 'a table away'.

Here's a feature about a detox programme run by Buddhist monks in Thailand.

> It's a tidal wave of puke. Like a line of wells simultaneously striking oil, fountains of sick erupt from the mouths of the four drug addicts. The clear fluid arcs four feet through the air and splatters the earth before the kneeling junkies.
> *Maxim*

Targeted at *Maxim*'s body-function-obsessed readers. Visual rather than smell-oriented, thank goodness. Lots of movement words: sick 'erupts', fluid 'arcs' and 'splatters'. Keeps to the vernacular with 'puke' and 'sick' rather than 'vomit'.

> When the kid in the front row at the rally bit off the tip of his little finger and wrote KIM DAE JUNG in blood on his fancy white ski jacket – I think that was the first time I ever really felt like a foreign correspondent. I mean, here was something really fucking *foreign*.
> P J O'Rourke, *Rolling Stone*

Straight in at the deep end with a bizarre incident. Take the 'fancy white' out of the description of the jacket and the intro doesn't work so well – the blood loses its colour. Unerringly sets the scene for a violent review of South Korean elections, which ends with O'Rourke getting tear-gassed.

4 Question that buttonholes the reader

Designed to intrigue and make the reader think. The question needs to
be right for the readers, or it runs the risk of a 'couldn't care less' response.

> In the name of faith, hope and especially charity, will the people of
> Great Britain please put their clothes back on? This instant. Right
> now. Without delay. What we mean is, what has got into you all?
> Jan Moir, *Daily Telegraph*

A pleading, grossly overstated question, laden with religious overtones
and addressed to the entire nation, begins a feature about the nude cal-
endar craze started by a Women's Institute in Yorkshire. For impact it
relies, first, on surprise: questioning on behalf of faith, hope and charity.
Then follows an imperious demand that everyone should stop, repeated
with increasing, staccato urgency. Finally, with the readers paying full
attention, on go the brakes. The second question has the understanding,
sympathetic tone of a disappointed auntie reasoning with a naughty
child. The change of voice is achieved by the lively use of punctuation to
control sentence length and separate the contrasting questions, one
haughty and one matey, but both putting into words what the readers
were thinking.

> Even at this time of triumph it is important to remember the ver-
> ities of cricket between England and Australia. Winning is not what
> matters; the Ashes are about renewing old friendships in a spirit of
> sporting endeavour between two nations with a common bond.
> But, by God, isn't it great to beat the bastards?
> Matthew Engel, *Guardian*

The question is at the end but it's worth waiting for. Throughout it's the
tone of voice that does it. At the start, mouthing plummy, treacly plat-
itudes commonly employed to make defeat more acceptable: 'the verities
of cricket' . . . 'winning is not what matters' . . . 'renewing old friendships
in a spirit of sporting endeavour'. Then suddenly there's a whoop of joy as
the writer scents blood: 'Isn't it great to beat the bastards?' Again, the
punch word in the punch position.

> Do you have an annual appraisal system? Why? Before expending
> energy on a process so complicated and potentially controversial,
> it makes sense to ask what you hope to achieve. Most businesses
> do not know why they have one. They just do.
> *Accountancy*

Barristers, it's said, ask witnesses questions in court only when they know what the answer will be. Writers can't be certain how readers will reply. One device is the immediate follow-up question. The joy here is that whether the answer to the first is Yes or No, the second question is still valid. Great final sentence, making the writer's point with the print equivalent of a despairing shrug of the shoulders.

5 Quote

The most controversial of intro types. Variously damned and dismissed as lazy and/or confusing for the reader, and typographically difficult for the sub. In its favour: a good quote can be very effective and, if accompanied by a whopping big picture of the subject, it's a strange reader who would be confused. Best used sparingly. The prejudice against quotes is rooted more strongly in newspapers than magazines.

> 'I think it's safe to say that no one has ever called Rupert Murdoch a tree hugger,' said Michael Bloomberg, the mayor of New York, in a speech the other day. Yet Murdoch had committed his companies 'to a major sustainability initiative' that would dramatically reduce their carbon emissions.
> Alexander Chancellor, *Guardian*

Opens with an entertaining quote. The reaction is to read on to mock (most *Guardian* readers?) or marvel. Then comes the shock: Murdoch is thinking about global warming. What is he up to?

> 'Sophisticated nursery food' is how Mark Hix, chef-director of Caprice Holdings, described the menu offering of the 60-year-old restaurant Le Caprice. 'It's not the kind of food you think long and hard about. You can eat it with a fork while you're doing business.'
> Tom Vaughan, *Caterer and Hotelkeeper*

One of the most famous old restaurants of London and here, from the chef-director's mouth, is the entertaining truth, valuable for b2b readers – a dead simple and highly effective way to keep a certain type of customer happy: think about their priorities and make life easy for them.

One unusual way to start with a quote. Leave out the quote marks.

> I'm getting a bit sick of your apoplectic roarings, wrote a male reader last week.

> I do seem to have been rumbling of late like a 15-stone belligerent battle-axe, so this week I will enchant, enslave and delight you with something merry and light like marital rows.
> Lynda Lee-Potter, *Daily Mail*

To end with, an example of how to use a torrent of quotes:

> Gillian Helfgott, wife of the controversial pianist David Helfgott, says she doesn't give a hoot about the critics. Not a hoot. In fact she spends an hour telling me she doesn't give a hoot. During which time it becomes quite clear that she gives many hoots. She loathes them, despises them, detests them, thinks them spineless, passionless, loveless, worthless. 'You tell me, who has done more for classical music, David Helfgott or the critics?' She jabs her finger into my chest. I don't have to think too hard about the answer.
>
> It is midnight. It has been a long evening. But she is relentless. This is one tough cookie. . . .
> Stephen Moss, *Guardian*

Reported speech: a safer way to use a quote if you work for an anti-quote-start paper. This is musical writing that uses repeated *leitmotifs*. First, all those hoots, then loads of 'less/es' remorselessly piling up. The later quote lightens the accumulated adjectives, which contrast with the strong one-syllable 'jabs'. The final sentence of the first par works so well because you pick up her imperiousness, a feeling of being there, listening to her tirade, feeling the jab.

CONTENT

You've grabbed them with the intro. Now you've got to keep them reading. The care and effort that go into each word of the opening should continue through to the end.

Ways to write feature body copy are many, various and determined by the brief. All should include good, clear, lively writing whatever the subject and whatever the aim – information, description, anecdotes, quotes, comment, analysis . . . Other aspects covered here include practical advice on writing b2b copy, guidance for the innumerate on statistics, ways to improve wordplay and tips for would-be columnists.

Information

Well-chosen specific words are sensuous. Because they have 'handles', ie, are graspable, they reach readers in a way concepts don't. Here's a GP writing about poverty and violence in the East End of London. Correction, about his experience of poor and violent men and women. Correction, what he has seen, felt, heard, touched, smelt.

> When I came [to the East End] I didn't know what the bruised face of a raped heroin addict was like, or how children could be locked up without food, four in a room by a drunken father as a punish-ment, or what happens to a jaw when it is broken in a domestic fight and concealed. Now I do. I know what decomposed bodies of alcoholics smell like after two weeks, and the noises made when dying in pain and what happens to a woman's face when she is told her breast cancer has spread. I wish I didn't.
> David Widgery, *Guardian*

The rhythmic writing falls into two sections. First there's a powerful list of three – bruised face, locked-up children and broken jaw – followed by a short factual sentence: 'Now I do.' Next another list of three but all involving death – decomposed bodies, dying noises, woman's face, followed by a more passionate variation of the first coda: 'I wish I didn't.' The powerful images need no extra adjectives.

Even with much less sensational subjects, the advice about choosing concrete, graspable words is the secret of 'writing in pictures' because well-chosen words speak immediately and vividly to readers.

> It's 20 years since I've been in Moscow, since when the permafrost of the Soviet regime has melted and it's now possible to find a hotel without a concierge guarding each floor, but with plugs in the baths and a towel larger than a face flannel.
> Richard Eyre, *Guardian*

So much more powerful than 'vastly improved conditions'.

Some features are planned to be fact-heavy and the details you include depend on your judgement of what's interesting to the readers. Readability depends on how you present those facts: loosely packed or indigestibly squashed. Take this description of the special effects for the film *Titanic*.

> Chief among them, of course, was a replica of the Titanic. Or rather several of them. Even a 1/20 scale model was over 45ft long. There

was a 25ft version just to work out camera angles; there was one of the weed-encrusted wreck – which was hung upside down from a ceiling to make filming it easier. Shots of it were laced into shots of the real wreck.

But the big ship, the one that counted, was built along a sandy strip of beach in Mexico, and it was, near as damn it, full-sized. It must have been an extraordinary sight to see its vast, weird outline riding the waterfront sands. The Titanic was, in its day, the largest moving object ever made. The reproduction can claim to be the largest film prop ever made. It was 775ft long – 90 per cent full size – and for obvious reasons it had to be made able to tilt.

The real Titanic, best iron and steel as she was, couldn't take the weight of having her back end lifted out of the water; it broke as she sank so the reproduction had to be made stronger, because it had to be tilted and lowered dozens of times without real loss of life. Three-and-a-half million tons of steel and 15,000 sheets of plywood went into it . . .
Daily Mail Weekend magazine

Fact-packed – 24 by my count in the first two pars – but not dense. The writing is airy with hardly a backward reference or sub-clause before the subject. Most of the figures are round numbers, an aid to understanding in consumer writing. Exact numbers are wanted for b2bs, of course.

Even more packed and astonishing is this feature about a US champion eater. Most competitors are grossly overweight, but one of the most famous, Sonya Thomas, is surprisingly tiny, weighing around seven stone.

To give some idea of this woman's unlikely ability, consider just some of the records she currently holds: 8.2lbs of chilli-and-cheese-covered French fries in ten minutes, 8.3lbs of Vienna Sausages in ten minutes, 552 oysters in ten minutes, 5.95lbs of meatballs in 12 minutes, 162 chicken wings in 12 minutes, 8.4lbs of baked beans in two minutes and 47 seconds, 80 chicken nuggets in five minutes, 8.6lbs of sweet potato casserole in 11 minutes – and just for those people who were impressed by Paul Newman's ability to put away 50 hard-boiled eggs in the movie *Cool Hand Luke* – she has also scoffed down 52 such eggs in five minutes. It took Newman's character all night. Last August in Harrington, Delaware, Sonya ate 40 crabcakes in 12 minutes. It is that record she is here this morning to defend, or rather, to break. She has a plan to make it happen. 'It's actually easier if you can dunk them in water,' she confides.
Independent

Compulsive reading (except for the anorexic?) and all the more surprising because the first sentence is 112 words long, a length that usually guarantees turn-off. This list works because it deals with graspable specifics: exactly how much food she ate, what food she ate and how long it took her. Relentlessly, the stats pile up, with the info always presented in the same order: amount, food, time. The readability of this giant sentence illustrates the value of guidelines set out in *The Elements of Style*: 'Express similar ideas similarly: in other words avoid inelegant variation.'

Resist the temptation to use bullet points here because though something would be won – probably an immediate appreciation of her gargantuan achievements – something would be lost: that uncomfortable feeling reached as the sentence ends, after fact after fact, stat after stat has piled up and the reader feels very bloated indeed.

Here's a b2b feature from *Drapers*, the fashion business magazine. It's their regular weekly 'Indicator' slot relating to sales and trends. The week's subject was shoes (footwear to *Drapers*' readers).

> Women's mainstream footwear retailers are hedging their bets against a rainy spring next year, despite a positive week of trading. The independents surveyed for this week's 'Indicator' were holding back an average of 25% of their spring budget . . . until closer to the season.
>
> Following a pattern set at the Moda Footwear show this year, which saw fewer orders placed at the event as buyers held out to order as late as possible, retailers were playing it safe after a summer of downpours.
>
> Caroline Turner, owner of Caroline Turner Shoes in Middlesex, said: 'I wouldn't say I'm being cautious – I'm being prudent. It's good to have a bit of flexibility. I've had a great season and I'm only going to hold back about 10%.'
>
> At F. Dickinson Footwear in Barrow-in-Furness, Cumbria, owner Hannah Gummers agreed there was a lesson to be learnt. 'We've sold 60% of the sandals we sold last year, so we're going to buy much smaller next year. And if we have an unusually hot summer, we'll need to have a scout around to top up the stock.'
>
> But business was not a total wash-out, with 42% of those surveyed finishing the week ahead of the same time last year, and only 18% reporting a drop of sales.

Drapers' meaty copy, spot-on for targeted readers, offering revealing stats, facts, reports and future plans, clearly fulfils the editorial policy of keeping readers up to date with the latest trends and quotes from named traders.

A trade magazine for music teachers and students offered practical guidance to anyone starting orchestral work. Most orchestras – unless they are large enough to have their own library – hire the necessary sheet music. These scores, which musicians call 'hire parts', are often printed on poor paper and arrive tatty and defaced with almost indecipherable notes in a variety of languages. Nine aspects of best practice when marking up orchestral parts were described in the feature. The opening section was 'Equipment'.

> Use a soft lead pencil – 2B is fine, but 4B even better. You will be able to write more clearly, more easily. Hard pencils (any H pencil, including HB) require more pressure to produce legible writing, and this can damage paper. Moreover, their fainter trace can be especially hard to read under the glare of concert hall lamps.
>
> As well as a supply of spare pencils, keep a good quality artist's eraser. Pencil-end rubbers are fine for the occasional correction, but they wear out quickly under heavy use, and are more inclined to leave smears.
>
> Never ever use ink.
> Toby Deller, *Music Teacher*

Sound advice supplied with that truly valuable extra: reasons. These help to ensure that readers follow the advice and don't just go half-way, thinking 'Must take a pencil – but I haven't really time to go to the stationers, so any old one will do.'

Advice for swimming pool operators to protect their customers' safety was supplied for this b2b magazine by a barrister who successfully represented a lifeguard during an eight-week court case.

> Be much more willing to clear the pool. It seems common practice to leave this as a last resort. Clear it early, as soon as you suspect all is not right, or you cannot effectively supervise the pool.
>
> Ensure lifeguard training is carried out as recommended by HSG 179 and that your records are up-to-date.
>
> Follow post-incident procedures. Be aware that what you say after the incident may be used against you.
>
> Refuse to multi-task. Cleaning poolside, conducting pool tests and performing other duties while lifeguarding a pool could compromise the level of care you provide for bathers.
> *Health Club Management*

Clearly, succinctly set out. Full of valuable 'must know' information.

Anecdotes

One good anecdote is worth loads of description. After his death, Robert Maxwell, one-time owner of the *Mirror*, was described as 'The twentieth century's most monstrous confidence trickster – bully, braggart, liar, cheat, thief'. That's truly powerful writing, but surely the following anecdote – collected first-person and stored for years – is even more memorable.

> Since everyone else recited their favourite Maxwell story last week, let me give you mine. Shortly after he dawn-raided the bankrupt British Printing Corporation in the early 1980s, I invited him to lunch in my office. Still persona non grata in the City after the DTI's [Department of Trade and Industry] savage condemnation of him, he was typically bouncing back and wanted bank support.
>
> An hour before lunch he rang, down a suitably crackly line. 'I'm sorry I can't make your lunch,' he boomed. 'I'm in Bucharest.'
>
> I said I was sorry to hear it, particularly as there were going to be some other interesting people there. Who were they, he inquired. Two bankers, I replied, Philip Wilkinson of NatWest and John Quinton of Barclays.
>
> 'You've got Wilkinson and Quinton, have you? Give me a moment.' The line went dead, then he was back on. 'I'll be round there in ten minutes.' And he was.
> Ivan Fallon, *Sunday Times*

The anecdote swings along, describing what happened with no added frills except 'boomed' and 'suitably crackly', words which prove their value later. The end is beautifully judged. Good anecdotes require no editorialising.

> When Kitty Kelley was researching her unauthorised biography of Frank Sinatra she was told the singer had bought $200,000 worth of furniture in cash in wrapping paper from a Las Vegas casino – an indication of Sinatra's links with the gaming industry.
>
> She found a friend who bore a resemblance to Sinatra. Kelley then had her own hair done to match that of Sinatra's wife, Barbara. Together, Kelley and her friend went to the furniture store. They told the sales assistant that they had heard that Frank Sinatra had bought some furniture from the store. Indeed he had, said the salesman.
>
> Well, said Kelley, they were so fond of the singer they modelled themselves on him, right down to their looks and lifestyle. They

had to have the same furniture for their home, which was an exact copy of his. What did he buy? The proud salesman rattled off the list. We will take it, said Kelley. Because we follow his life to the letter, we must pay the way he did — so how did he pay? Which credit card did he use?

The salesman produced the payslip. Cash. Come on, honey, said Kelley, clutching her companion, we must go to Las Vegas and get the cash. They left the store and never returned. She had her story . . .

Chris Blackhurst, *Independent on Sunday*

The style here is speech reported, a device which enables the reader to hear the conversation as it might have happened, rather than reported speech ('Kelley then told the salesman that they were devoted fans of Sinatra, modelling their appearance and lifestyle on him and would like to obtain the same furniture that he had bought'). One tiny complaint: 'her own hair'? 'Her hair' would do.

Short anecdotes can be equally telling. From an obit of Violet Carlson, the Broadway dancer:

She once broke her wrist playing in the Jerome Kern musical *Sweet Adeline*, had it set in plaster and was back on stage before the end of the performance.

Guardian

Here's a long-remembered anecdote that perfectly captures character.

By the time he was two, Ian had already emerged as an uncompromising competitor. 'We had organised a short race among Navy children,' his mother recalls. 'Ian wasn't much of a sprinter in those days but this time he got out in front. Near the finishing line he turned and knocked down the other children, one by one, and finished the race by himself.'

Dudley Doust, *Sunday Times* Magazine

No surprise then that some 20 years later Ian Botham was hurling bouncers at the Aussies.

Quotes

What people say brings vitality to copy, relieves solid text, changes pace and offers a fresh or authoritative voice, allowing the interviewee to speak. In most features a quote early on acts as a 'kicker', enlivening serious introductions or detailed scene-setting.

Unlike news writers, who attribute quotes at the beginning or end of the sentence, feature writers – as ever – have more choice. They can break up the quote to show it to best advantage. The placing of 'she says', below, enables the strongest words to occupy the most important position in the sentence.

> 'The foot,' she says, 'is an architectural masterpiece.'
> *Financial Times*

Writers can animate an ordinary quote with description, movement and colour, which act like stage directions.

> 'If I was doing a 30-second piece to camera right now,' says the twinkly, rumpled man sprawled on the park bench, 'I would get into a completely obsessed state. No really, that's true.' He sits up and leans forward, insistent. 'I'm as nervous now, before every single thing I do, as I was the day I did my first piece of television.'
>
> It is hard to think of a less plausible thing for David Dimbleby to say . . .
> Decca Aitkenhead, *Guardian*

When a quote is less than hoped for, context can give meaning.

> Did she use memories of her father's death to help her performance? 'Yes, I did. Of course. You draw on whatever you have,' she says briskly. Silence. I can see her wondering if there isn't something more urgent she should be doing . . .
> Kristin Scott Thomas interviewed in the *Sunday Times* Magazine

Using other writers' quotes lifted from cuts can make a not-so-astonishing comment splendid. This is how Bernard Levin, long ago but memorably, greeted the news that Humphrey Searle's *Hamlet* was to be performed in Covent Garden:

> The news is welcome, even though from what I have heard of Mr Searle's music I am inclined to react as Beachcomber did when he read the news that someone (Janacek, actually) had written an opera to Dostoievsky's *The House of the Dead*. 'Stap me,' said the sage, 'I warrant there'll be some lilting tunes in *that* work.'

Questionnaires are a specialised form of feature where the interviewee (or their PR) does the work and gets the credit. Could that be why questionnaires are often disparaged by journalists? Studying the better examples provides a great guide to using quotes, shortened and pointed to maximum effect.

> *What's the worst piece of gossip you've ever read about yourself?*
>
> The *Sun* once listed '20 Things You Didn't Know About Barry Norman' and there were at least ten things that I didn't know about Barry Norman.
> Barry Norman, *Empire*

> *What would you like written on your tombstone?*
>
> Unavailable. Please try me on the mobile.
> Mel Smith, *Empire*

Comment

Lynn Barber's interview with a famous and elderly film star starts with a warning that the interview is taking a long, long, long time. She loves words and to push the message home dextrously uses one that has two meanings: one serious, one facetious. A joyful judgement. You'll know it when you reach it.

> It isn't as if he's particularly, preternaturally boring. I mean probably by the standards of veteran Hollywood stars, he's in the upper percentile of interest. It is just that he suffers from anecdotage, the terrible brain rot that overcomes elderly people who have spent a large portion of their lives on chat shows. When you ask him a question he quickly scans it for a cue word, feeds the cue word into his memory files, and then, zap, brings out an anecdote that has the cue word in it. Being an actor, he of course delivers his anecdote with every possible nuance of expression, animation, funny voices, gestures, pauses for suspense, which makes it take about an hour longer than it's worth.
> Lynn Barber, *Independent on Sunday*

More shrewd assessment. Tennis player Roger Federer answered 17 questions from Sarah Shephard of *Sport* magazine as efficiently as he plays. At the very end of the interview, after the last question, is a single word that says it all – and it isn't one of Federer's.

Question: As both a man and a tennis player, what is your view on the female players receiving equal pay in tennis when they only play three sets?

[*Squirms*] 'I don't mind it. Honestly, it's OK . . .'

Oh, the power of well-chosen verbs. Says it all.

Editors and feature editors rarely include passion as one of the qualities they look for in feature writing. That may be because the image of the tough, cynical, detached journalist lives on. But editors certainly rate it when they get it. The following feature was remembered 30 years after it first appeared.

> Women and children sleep two to a bed. Others sleep on the kitchen floor and in the sitting-room. There are about 120 people in a house suitable for 36. It is like moving from one sort of hell to another, said a social worker.
>
> That's one view of Chiswick Women's Aid Centre, Erin Pizzey's refuge for battered wives, which faces a crisis following Hounslow council's decision to withdraw part of its £10,000 urban aid grant unless it complies with regulations on fire, health and overcrowding.
>
> Erin Pizzey and colleague Ann Ashby say they will go to gaol rather than comply with the regulations . . . They will not end their policy of running the Chiswick centre as an open-door refuge.
>
> Ann Ashby reports the case of a woman who arrived a few nights ago: 'Her husband had pulled her trousers down and poured boiling water between her legs. He'd beaten her about so she had six broken ribs as well, and bruises and cuts all over. Her children were suffering too. She came to us, we took her to hospital and brought her back with us. She can stay as long as she likes. You can't expect us to turn a woman like that away.'
> Carol Dix, *Guardian*

The woman's story is told without the use of any judgemental language. The reader is free to decide. Calmly presented facts out-perform paragraphs of emotional ranting. The same goes for simple statistics.

> China executes more people each year than the rest of the world put together. Methods include lethal injection and firing squad. Amnesty knows of at least 1,010 executions in China in 2006, but a Chinese legal scholar estimates that about 8,000 people are

executed each year – 22 people a day. There are 68 crimes punishable by death in China, two-thirds of them non-violent crimes.
Amnesty Magazine

Statistics: use intelligently

Feature writers may be literate, but far too many, alas, are innumerate. They've become journalists because they were 'good at English and bad at maths', says Professor Roy Greenslade of City University. The result is that they're impressed by the numerate and tend to trust any statistics they're given. Quite simply, they don't check the maths or use their common sense. The *Guardian* admits printing more than 80 corrections relating to numbers within a period of six months.

Worse than appearing in the *Guardian*'s 'Corrections and clarifications' are mistakes revealed in letters to the editor.

> To the *Times*
>
> You state that '134 carrier bags per person in the UK per year would cover the planet twice over'. My calculation says that, if so, each carrier bag would have to be about 360×360 metres, or about half a million times larger than the ones I get. Waste is a problem, but let's not blow it out of proportion.
> Charles Armitage, London SW6

> To the *Independent*
>
> Something is rotten in the toilet statistics department of the *Independent*. If Nick Allen was impressed by the number of years Britons fritter evacuating their bowels he must have been even more astonished at the extraordinary daily catharsis apparently achieved by the Chinese. According to your article on Chinese economic ascendancy, 1.3 billion Chinese produce 3.7 billion tons of sewage a day, an eye-watering 2.8 tons each. I had been worrying about Chinese goods flooding global markets but it seems a more awful deluge is about to overwhelm us.
> Tom Mitchell, Surrey

Editors and readers value statistics because they come cloaked with authority. PRs know this well and so do politicians. In all cases, check. Don't accept statistics at face value. Think, question and use a calculator whenever necessary. If you're unsure, double check, go back to the source, get help from a statistician or contact organisations such as the Office for National Statistics or the Royal Statistical Society. For recommended contacts and books, see the Further reading section on pp. 183–6. It's important to know the numbers involved in any research (over 2,000 participants are needed to achieve a +/– 3 per cent accuracy); also to know the relevant definitions used. There's a theory that dubious figures sometimes come from pressure groups. For example, one much quoted 'fact' is that one in five women suffers domestic violence. This figure is apparently based on using a definition of 'domestic violence' as being 'forced to do menial and trivial tasks'. 'By that token,' concludes one critic, 'almost everyone in a relationship is abused.' Sometimes figures can provide a feature on their own. These 'statistics' were reproduced in *Private Eye*'s 'Street of Shame' column while the Mills/McCartney divorce was at the pre-court stage:

> £20 million – Heather Mills-McCartney's divorce, according to *Telegraph*
>
> £30 million – Heather Mills-McCartney's divorce, according to *Sun*
>
> £50 million – Heather Mills-McCartney's divorce, according to *Express*
>
> £70 million – Heather Mills-McCartney's divorce, according to *Mail*
> Private Eye

And some people still think journalism's a profession.

Wordplay*

Talented feature editors are shrewd and practised judges. They read for a living day in, day out, and quickly recognise writing that needs substantial work to make it acceptable or features that can be improved by a few swift changes. They welcome work that's lively, writing that's stylish. But they rejoice when they find a feature by a clever writer who can play with words.

> Wanting to meet a writer because you like their books is like wanting to meet a duck because you like pâté.
> Margaret Atwood, *Guardian*

* See also Chapter 6 Style.

> He [a politician] also oozes sincerity; his brow is so furrowed, you
> could throw a handful of seeds over it, and in three months' time
> you'd probably have a good show of green beans . . .
> Rachel Cooke, *Observer*

> I've always thought that journalism is such a loathsome profession
> that our coat of arms ought to be emblazoned with two maggots
> rampant over a bucket of sick, surmounted by a chequebook.
> Victor Lewis-Smith, *Mirror*

Three examples. The first, an unexpected, unreal comparison that's a powerful put-down. This works by choosing a word that's totally unexpected but linked verbally. For example, commenting on a politician who is quoted as 'wishing to run the country,' by adding: 'I wouldn't let him run my bath.'

The second example is a crazy visual suggestion that works by ridiculous exaggeration. P G Wodehouse was a master of this. 'Roderick Spode? Big chap with a small moustache and the sort of eye that can open an oyster at sixty paces.'

In the third example horrible, repulsive yet memorable images are topped off powerfully by the sardonic introduction of money with its corrupting, debasing effects.

Not every writer has a naturally clever way with words. The most able are usually those who read extensively and compulsively as children. P G Wodehouse is often cited as their mentor. For those who are interested, some 'clever writing' can be developed with practice. A great deal rests on the ability to conjure surprising visual comparisons, turning reality or famous quotes upside down or substituting one item or idea for another.

> Francis Beckett is the kind of biographer whose subjects find him
> either at their feet or at their throat.
> Michael White, *Guardian*

This works by the simple means of writing in pictures (feet and throat) rather than the expected conceptual non-visual words (praising or criticising).

> a master of evasion, more slippery than a Jacuzzi full of KY jelly.
> Richard Littlejohn, *Sun*

This description of Michael Shea, one-time press secretary to the Queen, uses a clever visual metaphor to get across that slippery judgement.

The television programme *Together Again* featured couples reunited after having broken up.

> What eventually emerged through the fog of cigarette smoke and psychobabble was the classic tale of a man who drinks to forget that he's stupid and violent, thereby becoming a stupid, violent drunk, and although he finished by promising to go on the wagon, I fear that what he really needed was a brain operation. Not a lobotomy or a leucotomy though. Just an operation to have one put in.
> Victor Lewis-Smith, *Evening Standard*

This fresh twist, following what appeared to be suggesting a known operation, makes a wholly different and telling point.

A Prime Minister supports (?) his successor:

> The words were warm but the body language was awful. He [Blair] umm'ed and ah'ed. His eyes flickered wildly.
>
> 'I am absolutely delighted to, um, give my full support to Gordon. As. The next leader of the Labour party. And – er – prime minister. . . .' It got worse. His teeth were so gritted you could use them on a snow-covered motorway.
> Simon Hoggart, *Guardian*

Two destructive pars that ridicule the then Prime Minister's body language. The first starts with judgemental scene-setting. Then his speech is cruelly deconstructed, using punctuation to transform and mock what was said. The full points – and dashes – reluctantly . . . stutter home the kill. The final unflattering and visual metaphor . . . how much lower could it go? Guillotine writing.

> The flood of complaints following TapeHead's comments on Richard E. Grant's performance in *The Scarlet Pimpernel* continues unabated. How, the cry goes up, could you be so lenient?
> Jim Shelley, *Guardian*

Old but wonderful: memorable and telling, the vicious and exact opposite of what a reader expects.

Sundry devices

Using one fact to embody a person or trend is especially valuable for short features, but the detail must tell. From a feature on the retiring head of American Airlines:

> A fierce cost-cutter who once saved $100,000 by removing olives from all AA's salads . . .
> *Economist*

Case histories are probably the easiest way to cover a complex subject in a hurry. They're quicker to write because there's no need for cross-weaving or smooth links. Another plus: the people interviewed are usually happier because they have a section all to themselves, as in this feature about couples married at Chelsea register office. Combining all seven stories into one feature would destroy the uniqueness of each couple.

DAVID LANGLEY AND REBECCA SWAINSTON

The odds were stacked against David Langley, 32, and Rebecca Swainston, 35, meeting at all. He is a lecturer in performing arts and was drafted in at the eleventh hour to drive a minibus of teachers to the open-air opera in Holland Park last summer. For the first time in his life he walked out of a performance and stumbled over Rebecca sitting on the steps. 'She spotted the bottle of Chablis in my hand and asked if she could have a sip. We sat and talked and I immediately knew I wanted to marry her. I proposed four weeks later in the Alhambra in Granada, and when she'd stopped crying she said yes.'

All their friends were amazed. 'I was the last person on earth who was going to get married. I enjoyed my freedom and thought love was for poets and priestesses,' reveals David.

From the register office the couple and their guests took a red London bus to a humanist ceremony and reception for 200 people in the Duke of York's Headquarters on the Kings Road. Throughout the reception slides of David and Rebecca, from the age of one, were projected on to the walls. After their big day, the couple travelled to Florence for a three week honeymoon.
Jane Simms, *London Magazine*

One way to celebrate an anniversary is to mark each of the number of years achieved with a matching story. Here, among the 30 greatest characters chosen to mark the 30th anniversary of *Star Wars*, is C-3PO:

You may think the *Star Wars* character you most resemble is Han Solo or Boba Fett or, if you lack self-esteem, Mouse Robot but – look into your heart – you know it's C-3PO. He's smart (six million languages), loyal (it is his intervention that saves Artoo at the Jawa sale-yard), sensitive, occasionally says the wrong thing at the wrong time but always has his heart in the right place (he offers to donate his circuits to his battered-up friend). C-3PO is redolent of *Star Wars*' unique (especially at the time) ability to warm up the coldest staples of science-fiction. In jettisoning his original perception of Threepio as a used-car salesman for Anthony Daniels' perfectly pitched prissy English butler, Lucas turned a robot into *Star Wars*' most recognisably human character, marked by universal doubts and everyday frailties. Doesn't that sound a bit like you?

DEFINING MOMENT Wandering around in the no-man's land of Tatooine, bemoaning his fate. Quintessential Threepio.
Ian Freer, *Empire*

Warm, affectionate, evocative and persuasive writing – provided you love *Star Wars*, that is.

When to ignore the guidelines . . .

Cleverly chosen practical information about the 10 best British beaches, selected for a variety of reasons – for children, surfers, rugged beauty, romance, etc – is more convincing than loads of enthusiastic quotes for undecided holiday-makers, because the facts in this instance are *exactly* what the parent readers need to know:

TORRE ABBEY SANDS, TORQUAY, DEVON

It's as though this large, sandy beach was designed with families in mind. Located right by the town centre of Torquay, it has plenty of parking, is close to the train station and just across the road from Torre Abbey Meadows parkland. Palm trees, evidence of the area's mild microclimate, give the approach to the beach a distinctly un-British, tropical feel.

The clincher: In a recent scientific study, Torquay beaches were proven to be the best for sand-castle building, due to their extremely fine-grained sand, which has superior cohesive powers.
Chris Elwell-Sutton, *RAC World*

One of the great tenets of journalism is 'You can presume intelligence but not knowledge', meaning 'Explain if you think the readers might not understand.' That guidance is ignored in the opening par below, with great success. The article appeared in the *Guardian* on Election Day, 2005:

> It was when Michael Howard shifted into the conditional mood that I knew which side of the Atlantic I was really on. 'On Friday,' he said, 'Britain could wake up to a brighter future.' COULD? You mean . . . it might not happen? If this had been Detroit or San Diego or Dubuque, incredulous staffers would have rushed the candidate off podium for emergency reprogramming. '*Will*, Michael,' they would chant patiently at him until he Got It. 'Never so much as breathe a possibility of defeat.' But this wasn't Dubuque, it was Ashford Holiday Inn, and the Somewhat Beloved Leader was addressing the party faithful on how, probably, all things considered, he might, with any luck, and showery periods on Thursday, even the score full time.
> Simon Schama, *Guardian*

Schama starts academically with a jokey first sentence, designed to hook both the smart set and the genuinely curious. There follows a quote that illustrates what conditional mood is for those who want to know. Memories of school and parsing sentences grab more readers. Then comes the eruption, a word in caps. So shocking there's a judicious pause. We're soon learning the American political style, dramatically re-enacted. After learning about US positive persuasion we segue easily back to a UK Holiday Inn and end with a diffident, faltering, beautifully written tentative script.

Writing columns

Columnists are in great demand because the good ones inspire or provoke reader response (see also pages 55–6). It's a difficult skill to master, much harder than it appears, and as a result the talented are well paid. Few journalists are likely to be asked to write a column early in their careers though many will fancy their chances.

Here's guidance from talented and battle-hardened warriors. It doesn't matter whether columnists inspire love or fury. It's stimulating the response that counts. One columnist on a Sunday paper inspired a tsunami of hate mail but when she wanted to move to a paper with more sympathetic readers her then editor begged her not to go.

Here are the qualities belonging to the four columnists whom Keith Waterhouse rated most highly. Waterhouse himself was voted by readers of an English magazine in 2004 as being the Greatest Living Columnist.

The valuable qualities are:

- abiding curiosity about the world
- forcefully held and expressed views
- healthy scepticism (not cynicism)
- a well-stocked mind
- the ability to write about everything or nothing.

Specialists' advice

Ensure you choose a subject that can hold the attention of someone in a pub; write conversationally; know your own argument and know your opponents' views before you begin to write; back up your controversial points and the more they diverge from what your readers believe . . . then the more facts you need.
Johann Hari of the *Independent* in *Press Gazette*

Include lots of facts, preferably things readers are unlikely to know; choose a subject that can be expressed in a single phrase; refine any argument until it is clear in your head; the opening needs to work immediately: it should affront readers, or make them laugh, or puzzle them in an engaging way; the columnist who does no original work is a dud.
Andrew Marr in *My Trade*

Stamina is most important, as is unflagging curiosity touched with passion.
Stephen Glover of the *Daily Mail* in *Press Gazette*

Don't get disheartened when you receive the inevitable hate mail that being a really good columnist brings. If you've made someone seethe, then you've made them think and that's your job. . . . Besides, the vitriolic ones make good firelighters, I find.
Stacia Briggs of the *Evening News*, Norwich, in *Press Gazette*

If you can make the readers laugh or just smile you've probably got their attention, no matter what the subject matter. But don't force it, never, never force it. Facetiousness is not attractive. Have confidence in your own opinions. Write your piece as if it's the definitive article. It certainly won't be but if you don't believe it nobody else will either. Don't be afraid to be controversial. Get under the readers' skin. You might annoy them but they'll probably come back and read your next piece, if only to disagree with you again . . . Writing a funny column can be the most difficult labour of all. But when it works it's also the most satisfying.
Barry Norman of *Radio Times*

Below are examples from two of Britain's top-rated columnists. First, Jeremy Clarkson on how he reacted on learning that Sebastian Faulks had been invited to write the next James Bond book. The second is by A A Gill – is he serious or making a neo-Swiftian proposal? Either way, their ability to grab, involve and ensure a response is astonishing.

> 'Nooooo,' I wailed, in the manner of someone whose daughter has just fallen from a cliff . . .
> *Sunday Times*

> I've always wanted someone to cook me a cat – not as a joke or a dare, or because of imminent starvation, but as part of a natural balanced diet and because they thought it tasted good.
> *Sunday Times*

Some columnists are so sharp they can entertain while giving serious guidance about how to be funny. Here's some 'advice' from a *Press Gazette* series called 'Tips of the Trade'.

> Any good column has three ingredients (1) a figure from an obscure source (quoted in brackets); (2) a reference to a current film; (3) a list; and (4) an arrogant disregard for the rules of maths. And grammar. With a mix of short and long sentences. For dramatic effect.

> As for inspiration, I scour daily newspapers and cut out any bizarre stories, particularly from overseas. I keep the cuts somewhere under the pile of old newspapers on top of my desk. This eases the panic over having nothing to write about when 40 minutes from deadline.

> I can't ever find the cuts, but knowing they're there somehow helps. And having an untidy desk makes me look busy and intellectual.

> Finally, always write to length . . .
> Martin Freeman of the *Evening Herald*, Plymouth, in *Press Gazette*

He didn't of course but he went on to write unkindly about subs, deliberately to make the important point that 'every writer deserves the protection of a good sub'.

So true.

STRUCTURE

Of all the stages in feature writing, structure is the most difficult. The brief may be the most neglected, but its requirements are clear and, once followed, provide a workable guide to what is wanted. The material gathered may differ from what was planned but the task of structuring remains the same: to select what's relevant and integrate it into a smooth-running whole.

This is not easy and short-cut solutions have been devised which bypass the need to learn to structure: putting copy into chart form or a pre-agreed layout – four case histories, an intro and a box, for example. Speedy, uncomplicated, but no help when it comes to writing long features. These are more complex than news stories and crafted as a unit. Paragraphs are not written in descending order of importance, cuttable from the end. The pyramid doesn't apply.

Trainee journalists naturally look for a formula to follow and many become uneasy when they can't find one to suit all features. They need to accept that solutions have to be custom made.

Editors whose writers use a single template soon spot it and sigh 'Here we go again, starting with a quote . . .' or 'Not another "There I woz with . . ."'. The design to adopt is the one that is right for that feature for that publication.

Where to begin?

Planning is critical. The more complex the feature, the longer you should take, making sure you are in complete control of your subject before you start. This enables you to get an overview. Begin writing too early and you'll find yourself wading through the elephant grass, unable to see where you're going.

What follows works for even the most complex subjects and ultimately saves time. First, go back to your brief. If you discover gaps, plug them. Then read and reread your research and interview notes until you have assimilated them. During this process, information on various aspects of the feature should be drawn together.

Take a subject like 'Successful fund-raising', with the angle 'making it profitable and fun'. Interviews with several practised fund-raisers might yield information on events that provide maximum income from minimum effort, advice on motivating helpers, tips on planning enjoyable campaigns, suggestions on recruiting committee members, crazy ideas that children like, warnings about legal requirements and details of helpful books.

These become headings, under which each fund-raiser's thoughts are collated. One way to do this is to use a variant of the 'mind map'. Take a large sheet of blank paper, A3 works best, and in the middle put a drawing or representation of the subject to help focus the mind, then scatter your headings anywhere. This is important because it liberates the writer from the tyranny of linear thinking. Ring each heading boldly, leaving plenty of space, and, as you go through your notes, add the most interesting quotes, facts, whatever, under each relevant heading.

When you've done this and taken the measure of your possible contents, you can then decide what you are going to say. To achieve this, answer a key question. How you phrase it doesn't matter. It can be any variation on:

- What's the storyline?
- What do I want the readers to take away from this feature?
- What's the point I want to make?

This focuses the mind and stops the essay approach, which starts at the task about to be undertaken. If in doubt, rehearse to yourself the subject, publication and readers.

For example: 'I'm writing a feature on . . . [insert subject] for . . . [insert publication] whose readers are . . . [insert a generalised description] and what I want to them to take away is . . .' This helps establish how relevant your approach is.

If yours sounds like 'I'm writing a feature on Lasham Airfield during WW2 for *Historic Hampshire*, whose readers are residents keen on local history and what I want to tell them is that many of the children of the men who worked there in WW2 are currently being made redundant', you're clearly on the wrong track.

Don't start writing yet

When you know what you want to say, work out a running order that will carry the reader with you from A to Z. To do this, look at all your source material, now collected under various headings and choose where to start. Bearing in mind your 'take away' factor, swap heads with the readers and decide what will best bait the hook. What's

- the most startling fact you've discovered?
- the best anecdote unearthed?
- the most astonishing quote?
- the most surprising event?
- the item with the greatest 'Hey, did you know that?' factor?

This is where understanding readers' priorities meshes with editorial policy to become invaluable. Once you have decided where to start – not necessarily having written the intro in your head – where next?

One way is to look at the ringed headings on your circled topics and plot the feature's progress with arrows and links, talking it through to yourself, so that the topics flow smoothly. It's important to keep information on topics together and not to jump around all over the place.

After being told this, an American journalist commented: 'My first reaction was "obviously", my second "but why didn't it ever occur to me?" and my third that it was one of those profound banalities "everyone knows – after they've been told".'

Some writers number each piece of research and then adopt the Chinese takeaway approach: 'I'll start with 19, go on to 45, 102, 93, 4, 8 . . .' This takes a very particular mind-set. Others go effortlessly from reading their notes to making a simple list. This is difficult, so be careful.

Well crafted, a feature can be a must-follow yellow-brick road; badly done, it becomes a confusing maze of dead-end, unappealing streets without signposts. The analogy is not far off the mark. Readers will follow meandering paths or four-lane highways if the way is interesting and well marked. They stop reading if confused.

Clive James's first job on the *Sydney Morning Herald* was rewriting 'casuals' (amateur contributions). 'Those months doing rewrites,' he says, 'were probably the best practical training I ever received. Gradually the sheer weight of negative evidence began to convince me that writing is essentially a matter of saying things in the right order.'

Nub/Dear Reader and context pars

Features have a beginning, a middle and an end. In uncomplicated features, the hook leads straight on to a paragraph which lets the reader know exactly what the feature's about. This is commonly called the 'nub' par or 'Dear Reader' par.

The copy then moves effortlessly into the main body of the feature. This can contain any number of sections, smoothly linked, which take the reader right through to the ending, which satisfactorily wraps up the feature.

But what if the feature is to aid understanding of the financial difficulties of, say, Nicaragua, or to explain new developments in leasehold property law in Scotland or to demonstrate the results of taxation inequalities on booze between England and France – all of which, stated like that, make unappealing hooks? A link must be forged between the hook and the 'nub' par or 'Dear Reader' par. Enter the 'context par', setting out any necessary background. For an example, see page 87.

Links

At all stages of writing, the way to ensure a feature flows smoothly is to go back to the top and read it aloud to yourself to check that nothing is ambiguous or mystifying, sentences are not too long and that the rhythm is there.

How to link is a much disputed area, almost as fought over as quote intros. Smoothly flowing copy is one thing; lousy links are another and very off-putting. If hooked, the reader will follow, no matter how acrobatic the leap, but you must establish credibility first.

Links are particularly necessary in 'on-the-one-hand-and-on-the-other' features. Here are some suggestions:

A more serious worry is that . . .

These measures will require careful handling . . .

The roots of the problem run much deeper . . .

Even if public confidence holds, the authorities face a tough test . . .

For more popular publications, links are simpler:

Meanwhile . . .

Anyway . . .

Simple to complex

Here are examples of structure, from simple to complex, starting with a first-person story, simply but dramatically told. The hook is a reconstruction of an armed robbery, followed by the nub par, clarification and confirmation that the hold-up had a terrifying after-shock.

Hook:

> Blink. He is wearing a black polo-neck and a black mask with slits for eyes. The end of a double-barrelled shotgun is inches from my eyes. He knows as well as I do that the glass between us isn't bullet-proof. My life doesn't flash before me but I see a clear picture of my daughter being told her mum is dead. That's all I can think of. Blink.

Context par:

> Every time I blinked that is what I saw. The flashbacks were horribly vivid. When a stranger points a shotgun at your face they're in control and you are left floundering. I floundered for two-and-a-half years. Every day I lost more control, and when I slept my dreams were full of monsters.

Start of main body copy. First section, retelling the event:

> It was just after 10am on a December day . . . at a sub-branch of Barclays in Leeds where I worked behind the cash desk. There had been two attempted robberies in the past two months and both times I was shocked but seemed to recover. The previous robbers had seemed amateurish – when I refused to hand over the money they ran.

> The third time was different. The bank was empty and I first saw the robbers when they were outside, running towards the entrance. They were wearing donkey jackets and black polo necks, with masks tucked into their collars. It was at that point that I pressed the silent alarm.

> As they ran through the doors they pulled sawn-off shot guns from their jackets. After I emptied the tills one of the two men said, 'Get the big stuff or you're going to get hurt.' We have small cash limits in the till but they wanted the big bundles of notes which were on a time-delay lock.

When they realised they were not going to get what they'd come in for they began to look agitated. A customer walked in, saw what was happening and screamed. The one who had the gun pointing at me turned to the other and shouted 'get her' but she ran off. They must have realised the game was up, because they ran out of the building to their car. The police arrived minutes after they had left.

Second section: the consequences with specific details:

After the robbery I developed this irrational fear that the robbers would come back and get me. I started having nightmares in the form of flashbacks – but it was not only when I slept. It could be just when I closed my eyes.

I became very remote and territorial: it was *my* couch, it was *my* half of the bed. I stopped showing any emotions to my family. I reasoned that if they didn't love me as much they wouldn't miss me when I was killed. Once when Emma, my 10-year-old daughter, fell off her horse, I couldn't cuddle her. Can you imagine what I felt like?

Third section: hope dawns:

After two-and-half years a friend told me about a programme at Long Lartin prison in the Vale of Evesham where psychologists were bringing victims into contact with perpetrators. I phoned the prison and said I wanted to go the next day. I'd reached a point when it was less horrible to face my fears than allow them to spiral out of control.

Walking into Long Lartin was a pivotal moment in my life. I was expecting the armed robbers there to be the evil monsters of my nightmares, but they weren't. As I started to talk about my experience I realised I was regaining control. They had to listen to what I'd been through. When the day ended I felt relief. I went home and slept and have never had trouble sleeping since. And, at 33 years old, my family life is back to normal . . .

Armed robbers are top of the pecking order in prison and will say their crime is victimless and paid for by institutions that can afford it. When they are forced to see that they traumatise innocent people in the process, some become very emotional, some even cry.

Working up to the conclusion: surprise, this isn't another first-person 'TOTTY' (Triumph over Tragedy):

I am lucky because Barclays has seconded me to my current post – working in prisons making criminals consider the human cost of their violence – and has agreed to pay my salary for a year.

The fact that it's taken so long to mention Barclays gives hope the ghost-writer is not in the bank's pay. The ending shows progress, too, in a change in the writer's attitude to prisoners.

> I still get emotional, even though the nightmares have gone. It was an event that changed my life and the way I think about criminals. I used to be a bang-them-up-with-bread-and-water person, now I believe in rehabilitation. I've never met the men who robbed my branch, but I know where they are and the sentences they are serving. I'll never forgive them, but I meet so many armed robbers that they've just become two of many.
> *Big Issue*

Context pars

Now to a more complex structure, which uses a grab intro that turns into a context par.

> 'Why in France are there no campuses worthy of the name, no sports grounds, and another extraordinary thing: no libraries that open on Sundays?' Thus Nicolas Sarkozy on his country's sclerotic universities. For an ambitious president, these might seem modest goals. But it is a measure of the universities' dire condition that they seem revolutionary. France has 82 universities, teaching 1.5m students. All are public; none charges tuition fees; undergraduate enrolment charges are a tiny €165 ($220). All lecturers are civil servants. Universities cannot select students, who can apply only to ones near them.
>
> The results speak for themselves. Not a single French university makes it into the world's top 40 . . .
> *Economist*

Starts with a dramatic question voiced by the French president, using graspable examples – campuses, sports grounds and libraries – to illustrate what's wrong.

Only then does the writer introduce the 'context info': eight worrying statistics and unimpressive facts. To see how well the 'people first' approach works, start reading in line 6: 'France has 82 universities, teaching 1.5m students.' Pretty stodgy. Then go back to the original version to see how welcome those stats are after you've been introduced to the dire conditions under which the students learn.

Below is a *Financial Times* feature, this time about important concerns which were *not* being discussed in the imminent Netherlands general election. Hardly a great gripper, so the feature starts with a lively descriptive/narrative hook, involving a corny play on the word 'fit'.

> Wim Kok, the Dutch prime minister, tugged manfully at a rowing machine. Fritz Bolkenstein and Jaap de Hoop Scheffer, his two main rivals, respectively wielded a tennis racquet and jogged on a treadmill. At an event convened last month by the country's heart foundation, each wanted to show he was fit for government.

Context pars follow.

> Fitness in the eyes of the voters will be decided in a general election today. This follows a campaign which has by no means quickened the national pulse.

> As a series of inconclusive televised debates wound up and photo opportunities dwindled, the lunchtime news on the state-owned network yesterday devoted not a moment to domestic or European politics.

The nub par follows: this is what the feature is about and why the reader should read on.

> But the choice the Dutch will make . . . will help determine the economic course of a core participant in the union. And electoral sentiment is shifting leftward.

Main body copy follows. Four sections for each party:

> prospects for the left-wing parties
> prospects for the free-market liberals
> prospects for the right-wing parties
> coalition possibilities.

Conclusion: Kok's efforts bolster his chances.

Constructed carefully

Now for a fairly complex feature based on several interviews and detailed research. It's about two teams preparing to battle it out at the *University Challenge* final.

It's a good story, well told. In order to preserve a realistic 'read through', the whole feature is printed here without comment, though paragraphs that play a significant part in the structure are numbered to facilitate later examination.

[1] Only a year ago, they were a laughing stock after slumping to the biggest defeat in the history of TV's *University Challenge*.

Crushed by 360 points to 40, Birkbeck College, London, found themselves the butt of student bar jibes and even elicited the sympathy of normally hard-nosed quizmaster Jeremy Paxman.

[2] Sixteen months on, however, things could not be more different.

On Tuesday night on BBC2, after the greatest comeback in the show's 36-year history, Birkbeck will lock brains with reigning champions Magdalen College, Oxford . . .

And the four-strong team are determined finally to bury the memory of that humiliation at the hands of Manchester University.

Captain Mark Conway said: 'Getting to the final has been an achievement but our greatest challenge is yet to come. We would like to silence all the critics who had a go at Birkbeck's performance in the last series.'

[3] Birkbeck is Britain's largest college for part-time students and all the *University Challenge* team combine full-time work with their studies.

Mr Conway, studying Classical Civilisation, is a teacher. Catherine Arbuthnott (Mediaeval Latin) a university administrator. Mike Austin (History and Archaeology) a chartered engineer and Neil Best (Art History) a bookseller.

Conway, 39, oversaw the recruitment of the current team. His predecessor as captain, David Allen, a maths student and trades union worker, had simply picked those who responded first to posters placed around the college.

[4] This year the selection process was far more rigorous.

Mike Austin, at 61 the squad's elder statesman, came forward after watching the excruciating previous year defeat. 'I just thought I could do better than that,' said Austin, who has provided a science dimension to a team made up of arts students.

All applications were thoroughly tested first. Then, when the team had been chosen, a secret weapon was devised to help them train – a mock-up of the famous *University Challenge* desk complete with the all-important buzzers.

To re-create the tension of the *University Challenge* studio, it was set up in Birkbeck's student union bar.

Test questions were fired at the team as fellow undergraduates stood around drinking beer and jeering at every fluffed question.

'It really helped sharpen us up – speed to the buzzer is the key to winning *University Challenge*,' said Miss Arbuthnott, a cousin of the Scottish aristocrat Viscount Arbuthnott. Yet despite many hours of practice, she admitted the shadow of last year's disaster loomed large as they went into the first round against Cardiff University.

[5] 'At one point we got stuck on 20 points and we were just praying we could get at least 45 points,' she said. But they went on to win and followed up with convincing victories against Robinson College, Cambridge, and Edinburgh.

The semi-final against Nottingham University was a tetchy affair. 'They were very smug and thought they would walk all over us. When they lost they couldn't even bear to shake our hands,' said Mr Austin.

[6] The final will be an intriguing contest of town versus gown.

Birkbeck, part of London University, was founded in 1832 at the Crown and Anchor Tavern in the Strand, when it was agreed to establish a 'London Mechanics Institution'.

The college – motto In Nocte Consillium, 'teaching by night' – is based in drab buildings in Central London and has spent the past decade staving off a series of financial crises.

By contrast, the Magdalen College team attend one of the oldest and wealthiest colleges in the country.

Its buildings include a historic tower, an ornate 15th Century banqueting hall and a chapel which is home to the famous Magdalen choristers and adorned with great art works including a Leonardo Da Vinci.

Magdalen alumni include Edward VIII, Princess Diana's brother, Earl Spencer, the historian A.J.P.Taylor, and the writer C. S. Lewis. Mr Conway and his fellow part-timers will have to battle hard to beat Magdalen's young bloods.

The Oxford team, average age just 23, have already chalked up the highest score in this series – 375 points – and hope to become the first college to win the title two years running.

[7] But win or lose, Birkbeck will have restored their reputation.

Mark Amado, Birkbeck's acting student union president, said: 'Last year's team suffered from stage fright. We trained harder

this year because we wanted to show that Birkbeck is as good as
– or even better than – other universities.'
Mail on Sunday

Why and how the structure works

[1] Starts with a very strong 'disaster' hook, reinforced with strong, emotional words such as 'laughing stock', 'slumping' and 'biggest defeat'. Introduces an amazing piece of information: Jeremy Paxman was sorry for them.

[2] Here's the 'Dear Reader' sentence which turns into the 'Dear Reader' par: what the feature is all about. Things have changed dramatically and 'the greatest challenge is yet to come'.

[3] The scene has been set and the curtain is about to go up on this drama. So first meet the college and the cast. This section describes the present situation, recalls the back history and reveals how the previous team was chosen.

[4] A second 'nub par' alerts the reader about the new selection and training process.

[5] Time to discover how they fared in the earlier rounds.

[6] This section contrasts the combatants: their differing history, location, alumni, liquidity . . .

[7] The end echoes the start but what a change of tone. This time the words and the message are positive. There's been a complete turnaround. The quote reinforces how proud Birkbeck people are.

Alas, Birkbeck lost – but won the praise and publicity stakes.

ENDINGS

Readers who find a feature's first par mildly interesting often sample the end before deciding whether to read the rest, so the last par grows in importance. A well-crafted ending rewards both the hooked and the 'dip in' reader by offering a satisfying conclusion, nailing the feature down firmly. Don't fall into the essay or speech trap by repeating the intro.

Features often end with statements or quotes; less commonly with anecdotes and descriptions; rarely with questions. Whatever the approach chosen, it should suit the feature, reader and publication. Concluding statements, for example, can be positive, negative, tentative even. They can hammer or thump home a point. What they should avoid is being timid or apologetic, slinking away out of sight.

The *Mirror*'s feature about Sir Alex Ferguson's dressing-room doctrine (pages 54–5) ends with a neat Fergie quote which encapsulates his practical philosophy:

> But the most important thing is to play a team that wins.

Often the most effective conclusions echo the start but show the reader clearly how much progress has been achieved, how much ground has been covered. Probably more than anywhere else in a feature, knowing about power points in a sentence pays off. The most forceful endings put the most important word at the end, in the final 'punch' position.

The feature by Sally Brampton (page 58) ends:

> But what pleases me most is that, for one whole year, I have not wanted to die. It sounds absurd but every morning when I wake up, I feel proud.
>
> I am still here.

A feature starting:

> My first instinct was that Judy Hall was barking mad. My second was that I would be, too, if I didn't get out of there as quickly as possible.

ends:

> I don't know, but as I drove away across the Wiltshire Downs I felt lighter and less sceptical than I had been four hours earlier. A ghost had been laid to rest.
> Annabel Heseltine, *Daily Mail*

Again, a huge change. The writer, who wanted to get out as quickly as possible in the intro stayed for four hours and left with changed perceptions.

Endings work well when they embody some conclusion reached during the course of the story that is of help to the reader. The intro to the following feature about libel lawyers starts with an analogy that all but the smuggest swat can identify with.

> Watching your editor read a solicitor's letter threatening libel is like watching your parents read your school report. You may have goofed, but don't panic – unless the letter is from [five law firms mentioned].

It ends:

> If more publishers had a bit of guts, a lot of these threatening letters could be stopped dead.

The feature included the information that there were a total of possibly 100 lawyers expert in libel law and that almost all solicitors' letters were uninformed posturing. Reassuring and helpful.

Here's the conclusion to the intro on page 60 about staff appraisal, in a magazine designed for busy top-level accountants.

> Appraisal systems are the last ditch attempt by personnel to get managers to do some (people) managing. The problem is that they give managers an excuse not to do it the rest of the year. The answer is not to spend money and time on useless systems but to insist that managers manage – and that they are willing, able and motivated to give objective, timely and helpful feedback to their staff appropriate to their level of readiness. Spend the personnel manager's time on reinforcing this, not on collecting bits of paper.
> *Accountancy*

This ending could achieve Stage 4 on the feature scale (see page 47) and produce positive action.

Readers interested but not hooked by the intro to a feature about John Updike, describing how he'd forgotten the number of his hotel room, might decide to check by scanning the last par.

> As I stand up to go, he does too, and abruptly catches sight of his underpants. 'Oh God,' he cries, scooping them up and feverishly stuffing them, with a pair of worn black socks, into his suitcase. 'How careless of me. I do hope it's not psychic litter.'

What was going on? Back to the intro at once.

EXTRAS

Backstories, stats boxes, sidebars, tables and panels may look like after-thoughts but they're now integral to many features. Most writers need to think about them, if not at the idea stage then during research.

Content and style are determined by readers' interests and the time they have to spare. For extras, writing should be more concise than usual, at times telegrammatic even. Easy reading is the key: short subject–verb–object sentences. Even subject–object phrases. Clauses should be kept to a minimum.

Journalists often give PRs a hard time, bludgeoning them for immediate help and offering scant thanks. Here's where courtesy and consideration pay off, as PRs are able to do much of the labour-intensive work, providing info for extras that might otherwise take lengthy dredging.

Just facts

Beautifully basic info: every word tells.

> Scandinavian Kitchen, 61 Great Titchfield, W1W 7PP (020 7580 7161/www.scandikitchen.co.uk) Oxford Circus tube. Open Mon–Fri 8am–7pm, Sat 10am–6pm, Sun 10am–4pm. Lunch for one with coffee and cake: around £7.

Nothing but relevant information, clearly punctuated. After accuracy, the most important thing to remember in boxes is intelligent punctuation. 'Opening times 10am–noon, 2pm–4pm Monday–Tuesday early closing Wednesday 10am–noon, Saturdays 9am–4pm.' Any more of that and readers will be lost. Here's where full stops, dashes and semi-colons prove their worth.

Collected and selected

An impressive 11-page special on Everest in *Sport* featured fact boxes.

FAST FACTS SOUTHEAST RIDGE ROUTE

From Nepal

Base camp Khumbu Glacier

First completed 1953

Popularity 800 out of 1,318 ascents by the end of 2000

Main season April/May

Cost of commercial expedition $40,000 to $75,000

Duration 60–70 days

Natural hazards Avalanches, crevasses, sub-zero temperatures, hurricane-force winds, icefalls, sheer drops

There was also a page dedicated to what happens to the body at the summit. Not attractive.

> Lack of oxygen to the brain reduces the mental capacity of climbers to that of a small child. Near the summit, the brain loses thousands of cells a minute. In this condition, poor decision-making leads to fatal mistakes. Hallucinations and paralysis through fear are possible.
> *Sport*

Large quantities of information: boxes and panels

A *Horse* magazine interview with owners of a livery stable, three of whose horses died after eating acorns, had five 'extras':

- fact box on the likelihood of horses dying from eating poisonous plants, including avoiding action owners could take
- illustrated panels of 14 mildly toxic, toxic and fatal plants (see below)
- fact box on ragwort, the commonest cause of poisoning; where to obtain free information
- small par offering free info on revitalising grazing from a specialist organisation
- small par on the forthcoming second edition of a book on equine nutrition and feeding.

> Yew
> Appearance: Evergreen shrub or small tree, reaching 20m and living for up to 1,500 years. Reddish bark, dark needle-like leaves, small yellow bead-like (male) or green pear-shaped (female) flowers in March and bright red hollow-ended berries in late September.
> Habitat: Parks, churchyards, broad-leaved woods and chalk downlands.

Effect: Muscle tremors, unco-ordination, nervousness, difficulty in breathing, diarrhoea, convulsions, collapse and heart failure.
Toxin: Taxmine, a potent alkaloid.
HORSE WARNING: A horse eating as little as 0.05% of his bodyweight will prove fatal.

Valuable, practical information for the over 90 per cent female, horse-mad readership. That 'HORSE WARNING' is a sure sign of focused thinking (though wobbly sentence construction).

Speed-read summary boxes

Despite having the most educated readers in terms of years spent studying, doctors' magazines often have features with bullet-point boxes in large type which repeat the main findings boiled down to a few sentences. These are the journalistic equivalent of 'executive summary' pars designed for hyper-busy readers.

Key points
- Conservative therapy in the form of physiotherapy by an experienced and interested physiotherapist is the first-line management of GSI.
- Burch colposuspension can give a 90 per cent objective cure rate and is the current 'gold standard' surgical treatment for GSI.
- Continence devices may be useful in the short term in women awaiting surgery or in the longer term in those not suitable for or who do not wish to undergo surgery.
- Newer surgical techniques may offer less invasive treatment but careful appraisal is needed before they are adopted universally.
Pulse

Stat boxes

The best way to make stats readable is to delete verbs, adjectives, adverbs, prepositions and pronouns, and put what remains under relevant headings.

Autocar's section entitled 'Number crunching' includes stats on the following subjects to back up the earlier reviews of their featured cars:

- engine
- power and torque
- chassis and body

- transmission
- suspension
- steering
- brakes
- cabin noise
- safety
- green rating
- acceleration
- acceleration in gear
- max speeds in gear
- depreciation, compared over four years with two comparable cars

Here's one of the lists: info about the Nissan X-Trail's economy performance:

TEST	Average	29.9mpg
	Touring	38.2mpg
	Track	15.5mpg
CLAIMED	Urban	30.4mpg
	Extra-urban	44.8mpg
	Combined	38.2mph
	Tank size	65 litres
	Test range	428 miles

Impressive, added-value info.

Bullet-point boxes in b2bs

Depending on the complexity of the subject, features designed to include helpful facts can often look and read 'slabby'. This type of feature benefits from add-on bullet point extras, as do less complex features where additional advice boosts value.

A feature for teachers about body language in the classroom included add-ons on clothes to wear, style tips and the messages colours send out.

- Red: aggression, danger or warning (think the emergency services)
- Black: mournful or foreboding (think funeral)
- Green: calm (as in nature and often used in hospital wards)
- Blue: inspires confidence (cooling, such as fresh air or the sea).
- Yellow: cheerful, inviting and comfortable (the reason why fish aimed at children is often covered in yellow breadcrumbs)
- Grey: drab or boring (the colour of old age)

- Orange: enthusiasm and vibrancy (think beautiful sunrises or sunsets)
- Purple: dignity and power (regal implications)

TES Magazine

Info boxes

Straightforward value-added specialist information from experts:

> Olympus' SuperSonic Wave Drive image stabilisation system uses motion sensors to shift the sensor in response to camera shake, the former cancelling out the latter, but it's a mechanical system unlike electronic noise-reduction on, say, a pair of headphones. Because it's built into the camera body, lenses can be designed smaller and lighter, and long-time Olympus users will be pleased to hear it will also work with older OM system optics via an adaptor.
>
> *Photography Monthly*

Sidebars to make a point

Just after his 'cancer of bent and twisted journalism' speech, a feature about Jonathan Aitken – the disgraced politician and former journalist who later went to prison for perjury – appeared in the *Journalist*. Alongside was this simple sidebar:

NUJ CODE OF CONDUCT – CLAUSE 2

> A journalist shall at all times defend the principle of the freedom of the press and other media in relation to the collection of information and expression of comment and criticism. He/she shall strive to eliminate distortion, news suppression and censorship.
>
> *Journalist*

After all this 'How to' . . . a reminder – always check. Always.

> The details of Derek Malcolm's new book [page 5, G2, January 18] were correct except for the title, publisher and price. The book is *A Century of Films: Derek Malcolm's Personal Best* (not *Derek Malcolm's Personal Best: A Century of Films*). The publisher's name is IB Tauris (not ID Tauris), but more specifically, the imprint is Tauris Parke Paperbacks. The price is £9.99 not £9.95.

Yes, always check.

THREE FEATURES

The features that follow are not flawlessly crafted exhibits from the Museum of the Written Word, reverently preserved under glass in subdued lighting. They're here because they work: the writing flows, the details are graphic and the words are well chosen.

National daily newspaper

ABBEY OVERFLOWS FOR COMPTON

Matthew Engel attends a service to celebrate the cricketer whose innings has left an indelible imprint.

He was not royalty (not as such). He was not a great statesman (his politics were a touch, well, simplistic). He was not a candidate for Poets' Corner (judging from his contributions to the *Sunday Express*). He was not holy.

And yet Westminster Abbey was filled to overflowing yesterday to mark the passing of Denis Compton. Two thousand people turned up; a thousand had their applications rejected, the abbey's biggest case of over-subscription for a memorial service since Richard Dimbleby died in 1966.

Dimbleby died at the height of his broadcasting fame. Compton died on April 23, aged 78. No one under 50 can even have any memory of seeing him do what he did best: play cricket sublimely, and with an air that the whole thing was the most ridiculous lark.

And you would have to be pushing 60 to remember his apotheosis, the summer of 1947. Exactly 50 years ago this week, when an Old Trafford Test was on, just as it will be tomorrow, Compton scored 115 for England against South Africa, an innings described by Wisden as 'delightful and impudent'.

That was just one of the 18 centuries he scored that extraordinary summer, when Britain at last began to feel the war was over. Compton was the embodiment of that feeling. And thus when the Dean of Westminster said that we had gathered to give thanks for the life of Denis Compton, it did not feel like a clergyman's phrase, but the literal truth. We were not just remembering someone who happened to be amazingly successful (the idea of a man good enough to play both football and cricket for England is now unthinkable), we were honouring someone who made an indelible imprint on the life of the nation.

Among the 2,000 were many you would have expected: dozens of retired cricketers, one former prime minister (no prizes) and all the showbizzy Taverner-types with whom Compton mixed so easily.

But there were hundreds of unknown folk, too, and some highly improbable ones – like Dennis Skinner who was on his way to the Commons, asked what the fuss was, and was ushered in as a special guest.

Skinner watched Compton play at Derby. 'I expect we were miles apart politically. But he was an adventurer, wasn't he? He took risks. He was everything that Boycott wasn't.'

The ceremony itself was fairly standard issue: I Vow To Thee My Country, Jerusalem and Pomp and Circumstance to finish, but all beautifully done. The chairman of Arsenal read Let us Now Praise Famous Men; E W Swanton, still thunderous at 90, read Cardus on Lord's.

The address was given by Compton's one-time Middlesex team-mate and long-standing buddy, J J Warr, who delved briefly into the treasure chest of Compton-iana. These tales mostly rely on Compo's famously casual attitude to everything.

'In May 1967 he announced he was going to have an enormous party for his 50th birthday. His mother phoned him and said: "It's a good idea, Denis, but you're only 49." It was one of the few occasions when he was early for anything.'

One did half-expect Compo to wander in at any moment, late and full of apologies. It could have been the young daredevil of 1947 or the old man – knee and hips crocked – leaning on his stick. He had star quality throughout his life, which is what brought us to the abbey.

The decision to stage the Compton ceremony, made by the Dean, Wesley Carr, appears to be part of a trend towards populism in abbey memorial services. Brian Johnston, Les Dawson and Bobby Moore have recently received this very final British accolade. In contrast, politicians are now usually dealt with at St Margaret's, Westminster.

The honour would not have bothered Compo that much. As Warr said, his CBE was last seen hanging round the neck of his Old English sheepdog. But he would have loved the occasion, and the chance for a last drink with his very special chums. All 2,000 of them.

Guardian, 2 July 1997

This is rich writing, covering a news event and adding so much more in background colour and detail. At the end readers have the sense of having been at the service. They know the hymns, the readings, who spoke the eulogy. 'We were there,' says Engel editorialising in a very un-newsy way, witness those rather intrusive early brackets.

Readers learn a great detail about Compton, his cricket (particular score on a particular date on a particular ground and the number of centuries scored in a particular year), his character and lifestyle, his sporting abilities, his friends and admirers – and also about Britain in 1947. Also, details of the most heavily subscribed memorial services at Westminster Abbey, names of recent celebrities honoured, the location for many politicians' memorial services, and on and on. Even two visual images of Compton young and old. And it's all wrapped up with a conclusion including an affectionate anecdote, the 1940-ish word 'chums' and a feeling of the Abbey packed with friends and admirers paying tribute to a remarkable man.

The structure is not the usual sequential approach, but proceeds at first by negatives, builds up his reputation using figures and a contrast with the Richard Dimbleby memorial service, describes his career, starts on the ceremony, describes those present including a quote from a surprise attender, gives more details of the ceremony, then covers the address, goes back to other services and ends with an anecdote and an affectionate wrap. And it all flows smoothly with the genesis of each par discernible in the previous one.

Weekly b2b periodical

PICNIC IN THE BEDROOM

James Thomas, 36, joined London's Dorset Square Hotel as general manager in November 1996. 'Bedroom picnics' are the latest innovation he has dreamt up in his quest to provide home-from-home service.

Two or three mornings a week, I wake up in the hotel. If I've worked late the night before, I might decide to forgo a battle with the Underground and grab a spare room. As well as being convenient, this gives me a chance to see how the hotel operates from a customer's point of view.

If I have stayed overnight, I'll enjoy the luxury of eggs and bacon –

and I'll always taste the coffee and pastries to check the quality of our supplies.

🕐 If I've come in from home, I'll get in between 8 and 9am. The first thing I'll do is read the night manager's book and check up on the overnight occupancy and room rates.

My morning will be spent around reception, chatting to guests, opening mail and speaking to maintenance and housekeeping. This is a small hotel – only 38 bedrooms – so my job as general manager is very much hands-on. We're all multi-faceted here. For instance, we don't have a personnel or training manager, so my job encompasses both those roles.

🕐 Every Tuesday morning at 11am, I meet with the other hotel general managers in the Firmdale group at the company's head office in South Kensington. There are just five of us, all managing small luxury hotels in London. The others are women, which is great because they're so chatty. I know that's a sexist thing to say, but I have to be sexist because I'm the underdog.

At lunchtime I'll spend some time in the kitchen watching the service. I'll then nip out for a sandwich from the deli on the corner. I could get something to eat in the hotel but it's important to get off the premises just for 20 minutes, especially if I've stayed in the hotel the previous night.

It's also necessary to observe what's going on in the local area. For instance, by going out of the hotel, we discovered that many of our US guests were skipping breakfast in the hotel and grabbing a bagel from the deli before jumping into a taxi en route to their meetings. So we've now introduced 'Breakfast to go'. Five minutes after ordering it, guests can pick up a Dorset Square Hotel paper bag – containing juice, coffee and a pastry – from reception as they go out the door.

🕐 About 2.30pm I disappear into my broom cupboard of an office to get on with some paperwork. This is also a chance to develop new ideas. It's important to be creative. You can't afford to stand still – it's good for business and it stops the staff getting bored.

My latest project is 'Bedroom picnics', a name that we're going to trademark. The idea stems from last summer, when I returned from the theatre one night with a girlfriend and we felt a bit peckish, but weren't sure what we wanted to eat. Our head chef, Trevor Baines, said he would put together a few nibbly bits. It was great – a selection of all the kinds of things you like to eat in a relaxed way.

We've now developed the idea for room service. It is served on a large wicker tray with a green gingham cloth – perfect for putting on the bed to eat while watching the television, planning your next day's meeting, running the bath – or even in the bath. We wanted to get away from formal room service and provide something that guests can pick at with their fingers in the relaxed setting of their room.

The contents must be simple enough to be put together in a few minutes, even by the night porter. A typical picnic would include vegetable crudities and a dip, a selection of cold meat such as salami, Parma ham and turkey, hot Toulouse sausages with an onion and mustard dip, prawns in filo pastry, smoked salmon, cheese, bread and freshly sliced fruit.

I am just as likely to deliver the Bedroom picnic to a guest's room myself as is one of the restaurant staff.

① At about 6pm I write personal arrival notes to all the guests, which are delivered at turn-down. We know every guest's name and what kind of business they're in. Every Thursday evening between 6 and 7pm, all guests are invited for cocktails in the restaurant.

② I'll eat dinner in the hotel restaurant – the Potting Shed – two or three times a week. If not, I leave the hotel between 8 and 9pm. By then most of the arrivals are in, the turn-downs are done and the restaurant is buzzing. Going home to Docklands is a great antidote to all this – I read or watch TV.

Janet Harmer, *Caterer and Hotelkeeper*, 11 June 1998

Reproduced with the permission of the editor of *Caterer and Hotelkeeper*.

The feature was accompanied by a Factfile on the hotel, including address, telephone numbers, owner, number of bedrooms and room rates.

This is a variation on the *Sunday Times* 'Life in the Day of' page. The feature profiles a catering personality by describing a typical working day which exemplifies many. It includes a great deal of valuable hotel information: staffing attitudes, how often figures are checked, managers' meetings, how ideas to generate extra breakfast income are developed, a new idea – copiable under a different name – and how to run it, guest pampering, etc. The writing is deceptively simple, mostly in the present tense and requires no links except the use of the time. The style fits the catering and hotel business: hard-working, gossipy, people-oriented and rather like show business with its search for the new. By the end, the reader has a very good idea of the hotel and its general manager, together with some new ideas to ponder and maybe adapt.

Glossy monthly magazine

I LOVE THE JOB, BUT DO I HAVE TO WEAR THAT HAT?

Uniforms have come a long way since the nylon overall – or have they? Getting your corporate kit on can provoke mixed feelings, as Kerry Fowler discovers.

There's something about a woman in uniform, whether she's selling a low-rate mortgage or serving a G&T at 30,000 feet. When they're right, the clothes inspire confidence: trust me, they say. When they're wrong, the company looks tacky and the trendiest woman feels frumpy, no matter how hard she tries. As Leonie Barrie, Editor of *Company Clothing* magazine (the industry's style bible), says, 'It's a very emotive subject. People who have to wear uniforms are acutely aware of others' reactions.'

Uniforms flash up all sorts of message – fear (ticket collectors and traffic wardens), respect (look how far Deirdre's 'airline pilot' in *Coronation Street* fell from grace when it turned out he was just a silk-tie hawker) and instant recognition of who's staff and who isn't ('Ask the man in the hat, he'll know'). 'A uniform signals competence, kindliness and a host of other skills much more dramatically than the way you sit or stand, or the expression on your face,' says Halla Beloff, social psychologist at Edinburgh University.

Granted, if you have to wear a Mrs Overall pinny your expression may not have the same radiance as the girl at the Dior counter, but at least these practical numbers keep clothes clean. Better still, they simplify life. *GH* nutritionist Fiona Hunter is wistful about the white cotton dress she wore as a hospital dietician. 'I had 15 minutes extra in bed,' she says. 'I didn't have to think about what to wear. I didn't have to spend money on work clothes and it was all laundered for me. Now I have a clothes crisis every morning.'

But isn't that preferable to getting kitted up to look like Nell Gwynne? Not according to the supervisor at the Beefeater By the Tower (of London) restaurant. 'Dressing up is all part of the job,' she says. 'Sometimes the girls don't like the mob caps, but otherwise they enjoy it.' And what of the message conveyed by their wench-type costumes? Surprisingly, she's never had a problem in all her 23 years there. 'The outfits are quite demure and the maids have to wear discreet white bras under the camisole. We do get the occasional enquiry as to whether we're a topless restaurant but, that aside, we don't really tend to get rude comments,' she says.

Confusion is much more likely at London's trendy Pharmacy restaurant (part-owned by Damien Hirst), where the receptionists wear Prada-designed doctors' coats and the waiters have surgeons' jackets. Are they there to give you a good time or serve up a prognosis you wonder.

No such mystery surrounds the tartan army at Caledonian Airways, who thrive on the attention their kilts and frilly jabots bring. 'Americans are wild about them,' says purser Jill Mellor. 'We get stopped on concourses all round the world by people wanting to know who we work for.' A hefty staff manual details everything from the position of the kilt pin to the tilt of the tam o' shanter.

'The quality of the outfit shows workers the kind of respect paid by the employer,' says Halla Beloff. 'What they wear has to inspire confidence. It has to be clean and decent, but it should also be up to date and it certainly shouldn't be bizarre. A bad uniform can put you in a bad mood and you need to feel good if you're interacting with people.'

Elizabeth, now a dance teacher, is still spooked by her experience in a Sainsbury's uniform 10 years ago. 'I can't express how much I hated wearing it,' she says. 'I looked like a bell – a big orange and brown nylon bell. But,' she adds, 'I did meet my husband while I was on the checkout . . .'

These days, many companies turn to fashion designers for help.

Sainsbury's has signed up Paul Costelloe, who revamped BA; John Rocha designs for Virgin Airlines; Bruce Oldfield has put together a range of workwear for everyone from nurses to chefs; and Jeff Banks has left his mark on Asda, Barclays Bank, Iceland and many more. 'It's a major status symbol,' says Jeff. 'Organisations spend a lot on graphics and literature and finally the penny drops: if you want to make a company buzz, make sure the staff are happy with the way they look.' Designers can't afford any catwalk preciousness, though. 'They're not just catering for size 8–18s, it's more like 6–40s,' says Leonie Barrie. 'They've also got to think about ethnic designs and maternity wear.'

So what's the secret of creating a classy livery? 'There's a reason why I say wardrobe and not uniform,' says Jeff, who estimates around 500,000 people spend the day in his corporate designs. 'The wardrobe I did for Barclays has a printed "flippy" skirt and shaped blouse that would suit an 18-year-old and a looser overshirt, pleated skirt and loose striped jacket that would be fine for a 55-year-old woman. (If you're over 50 and still feeling flippy, the choice of skirts is up to you.) But they still look as if they play for the same team.'

You can be a team-player even if you're not in front of house, and most occupations have an unwritten dress code – pin-stripes for accountants, chinos for computer buffs, Armani for media moguls.

Sometimes it's more prescriptive: at John Lewis, while the 'partners' (as the rank and file are known) wear navy and green outfits, the section managers select from Jaeger or Country Casuals, and choose from black and blue, too. It's like the old sixth-form privilege: instead of a boater you get to wear a skull cap.

London barrister Barbara Hewson conforms to a dress code devised over 200 years ago: 'Nothing much has changed except the price – the horsehair wig now costs around £340.' For fledgling legal eagles, though, it can be worth the outlay. 'Your client immediately knows who you are when you're in your kit,' she says.

The perverse psychology is that none of us wants to be a clone. Schoolgirls aren't the only ones to customise their uniforms. The Britannia stewardesses in the TV documentary *Airline* are asked to wear red lipstick to match their corporate scarf but, apparently, some slide down the spectrum until they hit pink. We all, it seems, like to be unique beneath the serge.

Good Housekeeping, June 1998

A lot of research went into this feature – 19 firms or types of business are mentioned and seven people are quoted – yet the whole flows smoothly. The writing is full of images, which is as it should be since the subject is visual. The lively quotes give insight into the subject.

The range of uniforms covered is impressively wide: from airlines to supermarkets, theme restaurants to posh eateries, barristers to schoolgirls. The quotes read well and are in different voices, suggesting that the writer can probably do shorthand and doesn't recast everything into her own style.

There's a deft touch with words: 'radiance' is used as a semi-sendup for a girl at the Dior counter, contrasting with 'tacky' and 'frumpy' elsewhere; the nutritionist is 'wistful' about the pluses of her old uniformed life. There's evidence of practical thinking and questioning: the sizes that are catered for, for example, and different styles for different age and size groups.

The piece runs smoothly because of deft linking and by the end the reader has been entertained, informed and enlightened.

4
Writing reviews
Harriett Gilbert

WHAT IS A REVIEW?

You are already a reviewer. Every time you explain to a friend why such and such a movie doesn't work, or describe the excellence of so and so's new album, you are in effect reviewing an art work or an entertainment: in other words, you are providing a critical assessment of it. That is what a review does.

A 'listing' is different. It need do nothing more than provide the reader or listener with factual information:

> 10.50: The Jack Docherty Show: with Douglas Adams

A review, as well as providing that kind of information, should describe the work and express an opinion about it.

WHAT DOES IT TAKE TO BE A REVIEWER?

This raises a fundamental question. Although everyone has a right to express their opinion, why should certain opinions have the privilege of being published? Why should a small group of journalists be allowed to discourage strangers from buying a book they might otherwise have read, or to urge them to spend their money on expensive concert tickets?

The internet, in its democratic way, may allow anyone and everyone to publish reviews of books, films, hotels and so on – and we shall return to this later – but professional, paid reviewers, whether online or in print, do indeed form a privileged elite.

One justification is that they perform a service. With so much art and entertainment to choose from, critical sifting is vital. Another is that a good reviewer accepts that the privilege of influencing strangers carries responsibilities.

The first is to know what you are talking about. You should, at least, have seen, eaten at, listened to or read the thing you are reviewing. It is not enough (as occasionally happens) to rewrite or even copy a publicist's blurb.

You should also know what you like, what you hate, and why. If, for instance, you find that all television programmes are much of a much-ness, think again before pursuing a career as a television critic. This does not mean that your tastes should be set in cement (indeed, it would be extremely odd if they stayed the same throughout your life); it simply means you should care.

There are some who argue that, more than that, you should be an expert in your field. There is much to be said for expertise – and, if you want to make reviewing the central plank of your career, you should undoubtedly work to acquire expertise in your chosen area – but a useful review may still be written by a thoughtful beginner or occasional reviewer.

In fact, a beginner or occasional reviewer can sometimes have the edge. As A A Gill has said about his job as a restaurant critic:

> In most jobs experience is a boon, but for a critic it puts an ever-lengthening distance between you and your reader. The vast majority of diners don't eat with knowledge, they eat with friends. They don't know what happens on the other side of the swing door. Why should they? Most people eat out rarely and with high expectations, not every day with a knowing smirk.

All reviewers should be aware that experience and knowledge remove them from their readers. For instance, because they experience so much that is bad – stuff from which they protect the public with their subsequent panning reviews – they should recognise that sometimes, in gratitude, they see the merely good as being brilliant. And their physical encounter with the things they review is rarely the same as the punters'. On the one hand, they usually have the best theatre seats, and can visit art shows before the public surges in to obscure the exhibits. Often, too, they receive advance tapes of television and radio programmes to watch or listen to whenever convenient. On the other hand, they may be summoned to *group* television previews, in preview theatres not obvi-ously designed to resemble comfortable sitting rooms, and critics usually watch films in the morning, in cinemas empty except for them and a half-awake scattering of their colleagues. A good reviewer should bear these abnormalities in mind.

Some artists find it objectionable for their work to be reviewed by non-practitioners. Book critics are, at least, writers. Some of them have even written books. But many reviewers of film, theatre, art, dance, music, and so on, have never actually practised the form, however great their theoretical knowledge.

Painters frequently grumble about their work being judged by 'art historians' (the scorn with which they utter those words would lead you to suppose they were talking of vampires). Theatre people are even more vociferous – for two reasons.

The first is purely economic. Every performance of a play is expensive, what with wages, lighting, rental of the theatre and so on. So, if the first-night reviews are hostile, companies cannot afford to continue performing to empty or half-empty houses, hoping that audiences will gradually be drawn by word of mouth. The second reason is that theatre is *immediate*. Film-makers, writers and painters, in contrast, have long ago finished creating their work by the time the reviews appear. And, although of course they suffer whenever their work is damned, the process is even more painful for those who must read of their failures and inadequacies when, in effect, they are still in the process of creating.

And drama critics can have an extraordinary influence. So great was the power of the New York critic Clive Barnes that Broadway managements are said to have scoured the telephone directories for other Clive Barneses, invited them along to opening nights and pasted their praise – 'The best play I've seen: Clive Barnes' – on the flanks of their theatres.

But still: does this mean that reviewers should also be practitioners? Many in the British theatre think so and, in order to prove their point, they once challenged the drama critics to try directing a play. A few accepted, including the notoriously scathing Nicholas de Jongh of the London *Evening Standard*. The resultant productions were widely agreed to be worthy at best, terrible at worst. While this may have gratified the challengers, however, it proved only that good reviewers are *not* necessarily good practitioners.

It is important to understand the limitations and potential of an art form – to recognise, for instance, that a play can do things that a film cannot, and vice versa – but it is not essential to be able to practise it yourself.

If the anger of theatre people is caused, in part, by the devastating power of bad reviews, it is also caused by a widespread belief (among artists) that the primary role of reviewers is to nurture and promote the form about which they write.

It certainly is an important role. Obscure bands; avant-garde artists; authors attempting new forms of fiction: without the encouragement and publicity provided by sympathetic reviewers, these would have an even harder time than they do gaining recognition. Art critics such as *Time Out*'s Sarah Kent helped to promote and explain the New British Artists. The theatre critic Paul Allen (also, incidentally, a dramatist) played an important part in ensuring that the BBC's coverage of theatre extends beyond London's West End. The marginalised, forgotten, unusual or difficult rely on critics to bring them to people's attention, to explain and to support them.

Well-established, commercial art forms are also helped by intelligent reviewing. Film critics such as Dilys Powell and Judith Williamson, for instance, have given their readers a deeper appreciation of popular cinema. But if critics did *nothing* but support and praise – or, indeed, nothing but carp and condemn – they would cease to have any impact. Their work would lose credibility and focus.

A paradox to be borne in mind is that readers frequently take their bearings from regular critics with whom they disagree but of whose preferences they are aware. If they know that a critic routinely dismisses or disparages something they enjoy, readers are perfectly capable of taking a thumbs-down as a thumbs-up. The clearer your views, the better you enable them to do this.

WRITE FOR YOUR READER

Centrally, critics must write for their readers, not for the artists whose work they are assessing (nor for fellow reviewers, however much they would like their good opinion). This does not mean that critics' opinions should twist and turn to make their readers happy; it means that critics should serve their readers. To do this, they must know who their readers are.

The readers of redtop tabloids, for instance, expect very few reviews – mainly previews of television programmes – but, what they get, they like to be short and snappy, followed as a rule by a 'star rating' (five stars for

'Don't miss it', one for 'Garbage', to quote the *Daily Star*). At the other end of the newspaper market, readers are prepared for longer, more carefully argued reviews. A lead book review in the *Observer*, for example, might run to 1,000 words of description, argument and opinion. (Occasionally, reviews in the broadsheets never get to the opinion bit at all, especially reviews of biographies by writers who were acquainted with the subject and choose to devote their space to reminiscence. This is not an example to be followed.)

Some magazines – the *New Statesman*, for instance – also run single reviews at lengths of 900 or 1,000 words. But most magazines, from the cheapest weekly to the glossiest monthly, do not. This is partly because their designers refuse to have pages packed with grey columns of words. It is also because, when they do choose to run a lengthy piece on the arts, it is more likely to be in the form of a feature. So *Harpers & Queen* might run a 1,300-word feature on a novelist's life, but its lead book review will be 350 words, with subsidiary reviews (not only of books but also of movies or restaurants) often less than 100 words. Even *Time Out*, a magazine of which reviews are an important component, usually runs them at between 250 and 300 words, no more.

The time your readers expect to devote to reading your review is important, but length is far from being everything. Tone of voice matters, too. Readers of style magazines, for instance, or of magazines aimed at young people, tolerate endless injunctions about what is fashionable and what is not. This is from a review of the paperback reissue of Armistead Maupin's *Tales of the City* in *19* magazine:

> The first book in Maupin's six-volume Seventies saga, and as all things retro seem to be in (again!), a pretty trendy tome to be seen reading on the bus.

Readers of literary magazines, to take a different example, enjoy being nudged by cultural references that it gives them satisfaction to recognise.

Understanding your readers' frame of reference is important. For instance, writing for the *Daily Telegraph*, pop reviewer David Cheal can use the phrase 'not with a bang but with a simper' confident that readers will know the T S Eliot quote he has distorted. He would probably not do the same if reviewing for *Top of the Pops* magazine. Similarly, when writing for the now defunct feminist magazine *Sibyl*, the literary critic Georgina Paul could talk of the 'feminist reappropriation' of ancient Greek myth; her readers would have known what she meant. But, had she been writing for a local paper, the phrase would have needed to be explained or (preferably) replaced.

Readers of local papers are perhaps the hardest to target. You know where they live, and should take that into account when reviewing things connected to the area, but, even more than with national papers, they tend to differ widely in age, income, education, cultural interests and politics. At least with most of the national press you know your readers' probable politics and incomes.

Magazines are more narrowly focused. They may, overtly or otherwise, be aimed at a particular sex or age group. There are magazines for people with such and such a hobby, job, cultural interest, religion, political affiliation. There are even magazines aimed at people of a particular ethnic group or sexual orientation.

Their readers, of course, usually buy a whole range of publications. To take just one example: a black British woman estate agent might regularly read *Estates Gazette*, the *Daily Mail*, *Cosmopolitan* and *Pride*. Only in *Pride*, a magazine specifically aimed at black readers, would she expect a review of a gig by the Senegalese musician Cheikh Lo to open as Diana Evans's did:

> The Jazz Café is brimming with swaying 'world music' fans, most of whom, it has to be said, are white. It's the same with most concerts by African stars. The question arises, why is it that black people don't listen to their own music?

Whether your publication's readers are black people, schoolteachers, film buffs, train spotters, gays, vegetarians, pensioners or clubbers, your review should recognise that fact.

Once you have established who your readers are – their likely interests, frame of reference, verbal attention span and so on – there are five further questions which, if you are to serve them well, you should ask yourself:

- Have I given the thing I'm reviewing my full, open-minded attention?
- Have I reached my assessment of it honestly: uninfluenced, for instance, by the fear of being out on a limb, the fear of upsetting the powerful, the temptation to be nasty for the fun of it, or the simple pleasure of kicking someone when they're up?
- Have I made my assessment clear?

- Have I provided my readers with enough descriptive and factual information for them to decide the value of my assessment?
- Is what I've written engaging – *to my particular readers?*

THE SCARE: *Chivalry.* This is the battle for The Scare's soul: righteous, inventive punk-rock versus gin-soaked rock'n'roll outlaw spirit with a one-way ticket to severe traction. From the moment 'Bats! Bats! Bats!' rolls in on a growling disco-rock bassline, we're met with the soundtrack to Iggy's own swingers party and it's stirring stuff. A good deal of its success is to do with the way Wade Keighran grinds the basslines like scars into the flesh of the songs, creating a pool of blood for singer Kiss Reid to writhe around in – himself some deranged hybrid of Mick Jagger and *Teen Wolf.* But *Chivalry* is about more than just cheap thrills. 'Eighty Eight' hides its fangs behind a rolling surf-pop lick and 'Swamp' sounds exactly like a song called 'Swamp' is supposed to. Order? Chaos? Who cares? In appropriating the most dangerous bits of everything The Scare have whipped up a fright to remember.
NME

BULLY BEEF AND BURGHERS by James Callaway (published by the author at 54 Swain Street, Watchet, Somerset TA23). Railway preservationists may recall the author as a volunteer stationmaster at Abergynolwyn, on the Talyllyn Railway; he has now transferred to the broad gauge and is a supporter of the West Somerset Railway. This, his second book, is set on the British army-controlled railways of South Africa during the Boer War and concerns the military and amorous activities of Captain Robin Goodfellow, Royal Engineers, and his misadventures with an armoured train nicknamed 'Bully Beef'. It is a good-natured romp and greatly assisted your reviewer to survive a tedious train journey.
Railway Magazine

HOW TO RESEARCH

The amount of research you need do depends on three things. First is the ambitiousness of your review. A 1,000-word review of *Lolita* in which you intend to discuss the general issue of movie censorship will obviously need more preparatory reading than a straightforward 200-word review.

Second is the amount of information available. To review a Patti Smith concert, for instance, you would need to become familiar not only with decades' worth of her work but with the accumulation of comment about it. The same would not be true for a concert by a new performer.

Third, and in practice most important, is the amount of time you have. Specialist reviewers never stop researching, if only because their present work is a form of research for the future. Occasional reviewers must do what they can within the restraints of the deadline. And, although it is impossible to know too much, it is worth remembering that knowledge works best as a quiet foundation for what you write, not as rococo decoration splattered about all over the place. Its purpose is not to impress the readers with your brilliance, but to ensure the solidity and soundness of your judgement.

The most important element in research is examples of previous work (if any) by the artist or entertainer in question. These allow to you to spot recurrent themes, obsessions, strengths and weaknesses and to assess the relationship of the new work to the old. Also useful are press releases, the internet (but do double-check everything you read there) and reference books. The last can be expensive but can often be found in libraries. For a list of a few that reviewers have found useful, see 'Reference for reviewers' in Further reading, page 185.

TAKE THE RIGHT NOTES

In most cases, you will have one chance to watch or listen to the work you are reviewing. Even with videos, CDs and books, although in theory you may flip back to the beginning as often as you like, in practice there may not be time for more than one go. So try to ensure that the notes you take are the right ones.

You need, first, to note those *facts* that you will need when you start to write: that the novel's narrator is a 60-year-old lawyer, for example; or that the opera has been relocated to 1930s Berlin.

Sense impressions are also important: the look of a stage set; the way the actor playing Hamlet uses his voice; the lighting of a rock concert; the dominant colours of a movie . . . whatever strikes you, make suffi-cient notes to be able to recreate it in print. And do keep *all* your senses alert. A film, for instance, is more than its narrative. It is also a complex of composition, lighting, movement and noise. As well as dialogue, the sound track will almost certainly have music on it, not to mention the sighing of wind or the constant throbbing of helicopter blades. The camera may cling to the actors' faces in close-up, or keep its distance.

Similarly, a dance performance consists not only of a sequence of movements more or less effectively performed, but also of music (or other sounds), lighting, costume and decor. Notice, *consciously* notice, all those things that are having an effect.

Quotes, where applicable, are also useful. Write down those that are powerful in themselves and those that could be used to make a wider point.

Finally, note your reactions. If you smile, cry, are frightened, are bored, put it down.

After all this, the next point to make is that you can take *too many* notes. Especially when reviewing a performance, if you spend all your time with your face in a notebook you are liable to miss key moments. So, be selective: note only those things that make a special impression.

Some critics make no notes at all until a performance is over, on the not unreasonable grounds that what they remember must be what most impressed them. If you trust your memory, try it. And, even if you have cautiously taken notes during the performance, it is still useful to write a quick sentence afterwards, to sum up your feelings: 'Pretentious rubbish; I couldn't understand a word of it', for instance, or 'Started slowly but, by the end, had me gripped.' The reason for this is to prevent you, later, from writing yourself towards an untruthful opinion. For various reasons, including doubts about your judgement, this is easy to do.

STRUCTURE

Magazines occasionally present reviews in a checklist format, as with this, from a column of identically structured album reviews in B magazine:

> **WHO** Carleen Anderson
> **WHAT** *Blessed Burden*
> **LISTEN TO IT** When you feel like being a funky diva. This woman has soul.
> **VERDICT**: Paul Weller produced most of it – that's how good it is. It took three years, but the result is a selection of the sweetest tunes. Carleen, you've been gone way too long. **A delicious, delightful 7 out of 10**.

More often, you will need to build an appropriate framework for each review.

To build your framework, you should first remember that you cannot decide on the structure of any piece of journalism until you know what the story is – or, more precisely in the case of a review, whether you plan to give a thumbs-up, a thumbs-down or something in between. You also need to know why you have reached this verdict.

Take, for instance, this short review of Simple Minds' *Néapolis* album (published in the *Big Issue*):

> Once masters of stomping stadium rock, the Minds have become a watered-down version of atmospheric U2 pop circa the 'Zooropa' LP. Although there are charming touches such as 'War Babies', the likes of recent single 'Glitterball' will soon have you dozing off. Things improve with 'Androgyny', but when they finished recording the album in crime-ridden Naples (hence its title) any decent melodies they had must have been mugged and left for dead.

The reviewer, Gary Crossing, is giving the album a thumbs-down because, he believes, it demonstrates how musically *boring* Simple Minds have become. The structure of his review depends on this assessment. First, because he has few words to play with, he has ignored those aspects of the album irrelevant to his central point. This does not mean that he has suppressed the album's virtues; merely that he has put to one side those ingredients he considers peripheral: here, for example, the musicians' technical ability.

Second, to show the extent of his disappointment, he opens by reminding his readers that the band were once 'masters of stomping stadium rock'.

Then, what little praise he has to offer is sandwiched in the middle of the piece, the place where it has the least impact. The opening and closing sentences talk of 'watered-down' and 'left for dead'.

Crucial to the structure of reviews is the way in which you arrange your blocks of positive and negative comment. The worst solution, because it leaves your readers feeling dizzy, is to zigzag from one to the other throughout the review: 'This is great, but on the other hand, but then again, but then again . . . ' It is clearer to have substantial blocks of points in favour and points against.

For instance, if you are reviewing a novel, it is best to avoid slaloming your way around every single aspect of the book – plot, characters, style, form, message, and so on – allocating plus and minus points to each. Instead, you should first put aside the least significant or interesting aspects, then, with what you have left, create solid building blocks of praise and condemnation, regardless of the aspect being praised or condemned. Thus you might, in one block, praise a novel for its prose style, intelligence and humour and, in another, criticise its political insensitivity, for instance.

How you arrange these, however, can vary. Reviewing a book you enjoyed a lot, you might decide to open with praise, have a small block of negative comment in the middle, then finish with another substantial block of praise. Or you might decide to open with what you think is wrong with it (but expressing it in such a way that your readers can guess a 'but' is coming), then move into a substantial block of praise that continues to the end. Or, if what you dislike is trivial, you could position the negative comment as a fleeting parenthesis at the end: 'The novel may lack the full-throttle pace and finely tuned plotting of its predecessor, but the raucous humour is still firing on all cylinders.'

You will also need to decide where to place the basic factual information. Depending on the convention of your newspaper or magazine, some of this may be given, as a matter of course, at the top of the review. Reviews of single books, for instance, will usually begin with the title, the name of the author(s), the publisher and price. But this still may not be enough. Readers seeing: 'Déjà Dead by Kathy Reich (Heinemann £10)' will not immediately know who Reich is, whether her book is non-fiction or fiction, or what its subject matter is. You need to tell them. The question is, when?

The answer is, pretty quickly. This need not necessarily mean in the opening sentence or paragraph (see 'Intros', below) but certainly before you proceed with any kind of detailed criticism.

Extra thought is needed if you are writing a round-up review: of the highlights from last night's television, the month's new movies, the best in recent science fiction or whatever. For this, you will need to consider how to make the elements work together, including the order in which they should be placed.

Where order is concerned, there are two straightforward solutions. You could either start with the programme, film or novel you liked most, allocating it the greatest share of words, and proceed downwards (in liking and word-length) from there. Or you could start with the most newsworthy, the one of which most of your readers will have heard, the one by the most famous artist, and, again, work downwards from there.

But these are not the only options. To take just one example: you might choose to allocate the greatest share of words to the programme, film or novel you most hated. If that seems appropriate, do it.

The other question is how to link the disparate elements of the review. If an overall theme suggests itself, pick it up and run with it. If, however, the works have little in common, then rather than try to crush them into a framework in which they are uncomfortable you might prefer to use some kind of link to attach one review to the next. For instance, in a round-up review of movies in the *Observer*, Philip French finds a link like this. First, he ends his review of a heist thriller called *The Lookout*:

> As with *Fargo*, the snow is thick on the ground and ends up soaked with blood. It's a competent film, and Jeff Daniels is, as always, first rate as the hero's blind flatmate.

Then he moves to his next review:

> There is even more blood and far more snow in *30 Days of Night*, a horror movie set in northern Alaska, starring Danny Huston as the leader of a pack of carnivorous vampires speaking some Transylvanian dialect.

If there are neither obvious links nor any obvious common theme, it is usually best not to push it. Simply type a full stop after one review, breathe, then proceed to the next.

PAST OR PRESENT TENSE?

Before you start writing, there is one small grammatical question to consider. Should you use the past tense or the present? The rule is more or less simple. Events that will have come and gone by the time the review is published – one-off concerts, for instance, or television or radio programmes – are usually described in the past tense:

> As adroitly as a snake charmer coaxing a sleepy cobra from its basket, he *persuaded* 98-year-old Frances Partridge, the last of the Bloomsbury group, to talk about her marriage. [My italics]
> Sue Arnold reviewing a programme in Michael Berkeley's Radio 3 series *Private Passions* in the *Observer*

The past tense could also be appropriate to describe an event at which something took place that will probably not be repeated: a performance of a play in which an understudy took over to rapturous applause, for instance.

Otherwise, the convention is to use the present tense:

> It's 1970 and the streets are thick with chaos during a state of emergency declared by General Franco's right-wing regime. En route to hospital, a prostitute *gives* birth on a bus . . . [My italics]
> Martin Aston reviewing Pedro Almodóvar's movie *Live Flesh* in *Neon*

INTROS

As with features, there are no rules about how a review should open – except that, as with all journalism, the words should snatch the reader's attention and be relevant, directly or obliquely, to the main point you intend to make. There are, however, a number of tried and tested formulas.

The most straightforward is to step straight in with the basic factual information referred to in 'Structure' above. Thus John Dugdale, reviewing a batch of crime novels in the *Sunday Times*, opens one review like this:

> Set in the winter of 1586–7, Patricia Finney's *Unicorn's Blood* asks why the Virgin Queen eventually succumbed to her advisers' pressure to execute Mary, Queen of Scots, and hypothesises that spymaster Walsingham blackmailed her after acquiring a confessional youthful journal.

This approach could be deadly dull. A careless (or maybe distracted) sub once changed a reviewer's opening sentence from 'This is an historical novel about historical novels' to the rather less provocative and interesting 'This is an historical novel.' But starting with the basic information works when it is unusual or arresting: in John Dugdale's case, first because thrillers are not often set in the sixteenth century; second because of the widespread fascination with Mary, Queen of Scots. Describing Walsingham as a 'spymaster' also attracts attention. Calling him 'secretary of state', although no less truthful, would be less arresting.

In the same column, Dugdale reviews the Kathy Reich novel referred to in 'Structure' above. Here, although again he opens with the basic, factual information, he gives it a critical twist.

> Kathy Reich's *Déjà Dead* is so undisguisedly a DIY Patricia Cornwell novel that part of the considerable enjoyment of reading it lies in ticking off the formulaic features.

Crime-fiction fans will immediately know what a Patricia Cornwell novel is: will know that her regular heroine is a feisty forensic scientist who time and again solves gruesome murders before the mystified police can. Assuming that most of his readers will be fans, Dugdale has therefore taken the risk of using a form of shorthand in his opening sentence (although, later, he does go on to explain more fully what he means). But the main point to note is that he has judged the novel's subject – forensic scientist solves serial murder – too routine to open the review without the addition of that critical twist.

Another straightforward way to begin is with a summing-up of your judgement:

> This is a magical and magisterial production by Adrian Noble: one of the finest accounts I've seen of a magical and magisterial play . . .
> John Peter reviewing *The Tempest* in the *Sunday Times*

> One of the freshest-sounding singles this year has arrived . . .
> Matt Munday reviewing Doris Day's *To Ulrike M* in the *Big Issue*

> *Jackie Brown* is fun . . .
> Alexander Walker in the London *Evening Standard*

You may, however, prefer to create suspense: to keep your readers waiting for both the basic facts and your judgement. One way is to drop them immediately into the heart of the experience.

> Nine men packing shotguns storm the old house at the edge of town. They are there to rout out the women. Teach them a lesson. Kill them.
> Fiona Morrow reviewing Toni Morrison's *Paradise* in *Time Out*

> Inside the Roundhouse at Chalk Farm, shining like a huge paper lantern in the enclosing dark, is this truncated, spiral, vision thing, conspicuously clean, with walls in white nylon and a fresh soft-wood scent, strong enough to overcome, almost, the smell of old dirt.
> William Feaver reviewing an installation by The Kabakovs in the *Observer*

As long as the image you select is strong, readers will be prepared to wait for a context or an explanation.

Or you might decide to open with the visceral *feel* of the thing you are reviewing:

A dense, thudding read that pumps its message home with the deliberation of a master sound system . . .
J B Woolford reviewing Mark Hudson's *The Music in My Head* in *Pride*

Or – this opening is frequently used – you might decide on a teasing or provocative statement:

The charms of crockery can be overlooked . . .
Tibor Fischer reviewing Janet Gleeson's *The Arcanum* in the *Mail on Sunday*

There are not enough sounds on the stage nowadays.
Susannah Clapp reviewing Nancy Meckler's production of *I Am Yours* in the *Observer*

Wife swapping will be the main topic of conversation at dinner parties this month.
Charlie Higson reviewing Ang Lee's *The Ice Storm* in *Red*

Or you might start with a relevant anecdote, personal or otherwise:

Nobody, it seems, bothers to read *Ulysses* nowadays. On a recent *Tea Junction* on Radio 4, the novelist Michael Dobbs remarked that he had yet to meet anyone who had finished it.
John Carey reviewing *James Joyce and Censorship* in the *Sunday Times*

I have come away from gigs exhilarated. I have come away from gigs disappointed. I've even come away from gigs held in a headlock by bouncers.
Barbara Ellen reviewing a Cornershop concert in the *Observer*

Jokes, quotes, questions: a review may begin with any of these. Sooner rather than later, however, you must get round to telling the reader *what* it is you are reviewing.

HOW TO EXPRESS YOUR OPINION

You have written the opening paragraph. Either in it, or shortly after, you have explained what it is you are reviewing. Now for the bulk of the review.

Perhaps the most important point to consider as you continue writing is the need to justify your assertions with illustration, explanation or argument. Except when the word-length is really tight, it is not enough to declare baldly that such-and-such a movie is 'funny'. You need to quote lines or describe a scene illustrating the funniness. The reasons for this are several. First, an example is usually more vivid to read than a simple statement. Second, you may find that, when you search for a suitable example, you are forced to reconsider, modify or even change your assertion.

Third, you owe it to the reader and the work you are reviewing. However informed or intelligent your opinions, you must never believe they are absolute. So, by describing what you find funny, you allow room for readers to conclude that your sense of humour and theirs are different. Similarly, were you to decide that a book was 'a load of macho nonsense', you would need to provide enough evidence of this for your readers to calculate to what extent your idea of nonsense corresponds with theirs.

Should you, therefore, keep repeating 'In my opinion' or 'I felt'? No: a review is transparently an expression of the writer's opinion. You may need to declare an interest. You should, for instance, make it clear if the director of the play you are reviewing is your mother. Or, if reviewing a collection of gay erotic poetry, you might well conclude that your sexuality needed spelling out (even your sex, if your by-line left that ambiguous). But to keep insisting 'This is just my opinion' is redundant and faintly annoying.

Next: avoid empty adjectives. 'Brilliant', 'beautiful', 'awful' and so on are the sounds of someone flailing in the dark. Consider *why* you think something is awful (or brilliant, or beautiful or whatever), then tell your readers.

You can even convey a judgement through description alone. Take, for instance, this sentence from a Nicola Barker restaurant review in the *Observer*: 'The meal begins with tubs of steaming hot, ripe-as-all-hell tomato and nippy mint soup with chunks of butter-drenched walnut bread.' There is no need for Barker to add that the soup tasted delicious. The description has made that clear.

Praise is a delight to receive but not easy to give. Even experienced critics, reviewing something they have loved, are prone to lose themselves and their readers in a mist of vacuous superlatives. The solution is to be as clear, precise and specific as you can – taking the time to analyse exactly what it was that gave you pleasure.

That said, it is widely agreed that praise is harder to write than knocking copy. A good insult springs from the fingers with such a satisfying elegance. Consider how gratified Mary McCarthy must have felt as she typed this condemnation of fellow writer Lillian Hellman:

Every word she writes is a lie, including 'and' and 'the'.

Or what about this, from the nineteenth-century critic Eugene Field reviewing a production of *King Lear*:

He played the King as though under momentary apprehension that someone else was about to play the Ace.

BEWARE OF LIBEL

If you truthfully feel that adverse comment is in order, then by all means go ahead. But do take care that your insults are appropriate and relevant. Insulting a performer's physical appearance, for instance, is relevant only if it has direct bearing on the work. Moreover, as a critic, *you are not immune to the libel laws.*

You do have a defence to the charge, which you share with columnists and satirists. It is known as 'fair comment'. According to this you may, paradoxically, be as *unfair* as you want, so long as whatever you write is your 'honest opinion'. But this is where things get dangerous.

First, opinion is not the same as fact. You would be perfectly entitled, for instance, to write that the crowd scenes in a production of Shakespeare's *Julius Caesar* gave the impression that Rome contained only three plebeians. But were you to write that the crowds were composed of three actors, when in fact they were composed of five, you would have no defence to libel.

Second, if your opinion is way over the top, it might be concluded that it could not be 'honest'. Libel suits against reviewers are rare, but a successful one was brought against a columnist whose comments on the size of an actress's bum were judged not only factually wrong but far too excessive to be 'honest'.

Third, you must not be motivated by malice. Should your bastard of an ex-lover publish a collection of poetry, do not, whatever you do, review it. Were you to write that their sense of rhythm had obviously not improved, you would have no defence to libel.

The fourth test of 'honest opinion' is that you should be commenting on a matter of public interest. This should not usually worry you, since a published work or a public performance is obviously of public interest. But it does raise another, non-legal, question. Critics disagree about this, but to me it seems there is little point in slamming artists so obscure that, were it not for your reviewing their work, your readers would be blithely unaware of them. Would it not be better to leave them in the shadows?

NAME THE ARTIST

Condemning or praising, you should usually name the people singled out. This may seem obvious if the artist in question is a famous chef, the lead singer in a band, the star of a show, the author of a book. But it also applies to translators, arrangers, set designers, and so on. If you think the lighting made an important contribution to a ballet, name the designer.

For actors, there are two conventions, depending on the structure of the sentence. If it is structured with the actor given more importance than the role, then you simply name him as you would any other artist whose work you were mentioning. If, however, it is the role that has most importance in the sentence, then the actor's name is usually inserted in brackets: 'Ulysses Jackson (Peter Fonda) works as a beekeeper in the tupelo marshes of rural Florida . . . '

SPOILING THE SUSPENSE

At the end of Agatha Christie's theatrical whodunnit *The Mousetrap*, audiences are asked to keep the murderer's identity a secret so as not to spoil the suspense for those who have yet to see the play. Should critics generally refrain from revealing twists, surprises and denouements?

There are two schools of thought about this. The first holds that of course they should, that anything else would wreck the enjoyment of potential audiences and readers. The second holds that, since a review is not an advertising trailer, it is entirely legitimate to reveal whatever the critic likes. This is something you will need to decide for yourself.

ENDINGS

The end of a review is usually a summing-up of the critic's opinion:

> But if you admire Nick Hornby's grasp of the easy comedy of life, recognise the universal truths he divines through a pop-cultural lens, and appreciate the deft interplay between mismatched

everymen (the single-parent's kid, the thirtysomething loafer), you'll love this.
Craig McLean reviewing Nick Hornby's *About a Boy* in *The Face*

Something is badly amiss here, though, and it's the labour rather than the love that weighs on you at the end.
Anthony Quinn reviewing the movie *Oscar and Lucinda* in the *Mail on Sunday*

Like I said, refreshing. Just don't get too famous, lads.
Lisa Mullen reviewing a Tortoise gig in *Time Out*

This is not a novel to be tossed aside lightly. It should be thrown with great force.
Dorothy Parker

No rules dictate this formulation. But skim as many reviews as you like and you will see that they might as well. In other words, you may end a review in whatever way you see fit but, if you find it *difficult* to end, then summing up your opinion is as good a solution as any. Besides, you will make life easier for lazy or hard-pressed readers, who know that skipping to the end of a review will usually tell them, if nothing else, whether to get their wallet out.

ONLINE REVIEWS

For an in-depth account of writing for the internet, read the chapter on writing online (page 132). If you want to become a reviewer, however, you should also bear in mind that there are two kinds of online review.

The first occupies the same professional space as most print reviews. Not only has the writer been paid but the review has been commissioned and overseen by an editor. In some cases, this kind of review will be the electronic version of one that has already appeared in print; in other cases, it will have been written especially for the internet.

The second kind of online review is most commonly found on retail sites such as Amazon. It has been written and posted by an amateur – by someone who has neither been asked to write it nor paid for doing do.

This *need* not mean that such a review is incompetent, ill-informed or generally worthless. Besides the fact that, from the retailer's perspective, it can be decidedly valuable – research suggests that 'customer reviews' influence online shoppers more strongly than ads do – many people who post reviews for free have expertise, integrity and passion.

But the status of unsolicited reviews is not universally high. The most prolific online book reviewers, for instance, may post as many as one review a day, which raises doubts about the thoroughness with which they read the books in question. And online reviewers have been known to puff their own products – books, hotels – under a pseudonym.

Admittedly, this has also been done by print reviewers. In the 1960s Anthony Burgess wrote a perversely enticing review of a novel that he himself had written under the *nom de plume* Joseph Kell. 'This is a dirty book,' he wrote in the *Yorkshire Post*. 'It may well make some people sick, and those of my readers with tender stomachs are advised to let it alone.' By and large, however, there are too many checks on the authenticity of print reviews to allow that kind of concealed self-promotion.

Although aspiring reviewers might want to *practise* by posting unsolicited reviews on the internet, such publication is unlikely to count for much on their curriculum vitae.

HOW TO GET IN

To become the regular film critic for a national paper or glossy magazine takes time, experience and contacts. The same is true should you wish to become a regular critic of any sort for a prestigious, well-paying media outlet. Such jobs are rarely available to young or inexperienced jour-nalists. Moreover, reviewers are not, in general, among the best-paid journalists. They get to see a lot of movies, keep a lot of CDs and books but, even if they have the luck to be on a salary or long-term contract, they are unlikely to become millionaires.

There is more bad news. Because so many young writers are interested in the arts, the competition for reviewing work is intense. But there is good news too.

Youth can work to your advantage. Most publications prefer to have younger journalists reviewing pop music and clubs. Less obviously, a literary editor may specifically want a young reviewer for a book aimed at the youth market or written by a young author.

Specialist knowledge or special experience can also be a useful spring-board. If, for instance, you know all there is to know about drum'n'bass, then you are in a stronger position than someone with casual, generalised musical knowledge. Similarly, if you have experience of accounting, snowboarding, being the child of alcoholic parents or whatever, you have a good case to put to a literary editor with a book on one of those subjects awaiting review. Or, if you live out of London and know your way round the local music, theatre, dance, club or art scene, you could be useful to arts editors fed up with trying to persuade staff journalists to travel.

The crucial thing is to keep abreast of what is happening in your chosen field; by and large editors know about the immediate and the mainstream. Ask publishers to send you their catalogues. Keep in touch with your local theatres, music venues, clubs. Read specialist publications. Surf the internet. Hang out with people who work in the arts. And, if you get a job as a sub, editorial assistant or reporter, but would like to be writing reviews as well or instead, make frequent visits to the arts desk to enquire about what is coming up.

Finally, although you should study the style and approach of whatever publication you would like to review for, you should never, ever, try to reproduce its critics' opinions. Your views, your take on things, are what matter – both to commissioning editors and to yourself. They are why people will want to employ you. They are what give you your individual voice. They are why you want to be a critic.

The ways in to reviewing may be obscure and hard to locate but, if you look hard enough, they are there.

WHY BOTHER?

The question is: why bother?

If you want to be a hero, do not become a critic. Creative artists hate critics. Readers delight in arguing with them. History loves looking back at them and sneering at what they got wrong. The only reason to write reviews is that you enjoy the art or entertainment form about which you write, enjoy being forced to consider why such a thing works and such a thing does not, enjoy trying to convey your experience in words.

If, when you were a child, someone had told you that you could earn money by cuddling up with a succession of books; sitting transfixed in the cinema; going to the theatre, the ballet, the opera, rock concerts; eating out in restaurants; watching television; watching videos; listening to CDs: what would have been your reaction? If you would have shrugged, forget reviewing. If you would have laughed with amazement, go for it.

TWO REVIEWS

Adam Mars-Jones reviewing Sebastian Barry's novel *The Whereabouts of Eneas McNulty* in the *Observer*:

Sebastian Barry's new novel is so full of magnetising beauty that it all but harasses a reader into submission. You can try to protest, to say, 'I'm a reader and you're a book, can we not keep this on a professional basis?' but the book won't have it so. *The Whereabouts of Eneas McNulty* is Barry's first novel for 10 years, and during that decade he has made a major mark with his plays, but in these pages he seems most like a poet. Many sentences seem actively to yearn for an uneven right-hand margin to point up their rhythms and designs: 'The cold desert in his mind's eye floods with the thousand small white flowers that are the afterlife of rainfall.'

Eneas McNulty is born in Sligo at the turn of the century, first child of a Catholic jobbing tailor, who met his seamstress wife-to-be in the asylum where he worked running up clothing for the inmates. Eneas is dispossessed for the first time when more children come along, but is consoled by friendship with an older boy, Jonno Lynch.

At 16, for no reason except the need to find a place for himself, and a vague desire to rescue poor, suffering France, Eneas joins the British Merchant navy. His taking of the King's shilling is not a political decision: in a striking phrase applied to the proprietor of the Great Western Hotel in Athlone, he – and the book which contains him – might be described as being 'above politics and beneath neutrality'.

After the war Eneas compounds his error of affiliation by joining the Royal Irish Constabulary and brands himself, in the changing political climate, definitively traitor. He isn't so stupid as not to know 'why there are places in the peelers when there are places nowhere else' but he can hardly predict the slow fuse of hatred that will follow him down the decades. Sentence of death is confirmed by Jonno, by the dear friend estranged. Eneas becomes a sort of sorrowful human comet, travelling in a highly elliptical orbit far from Sligo, in search of a place and an occupation – fishing, farming, digging – but returning at long intervals to whizz, grieving, past his family. He must part from the woman he loves, and never finds a substitute for her. Eneas may be named after a hero whose wanderings were ordained and finally rewarded, but he himself finds no home to replace the one he lost.

If Barry's prose is poetry carried on by other means, he is an unfashionable sort of poet, drawing images almost exclusively from the natural world, seen as a teeming library of images, mainly redemptive: 'The salmon is as clean as a pig in its nature, though unlike the pig it will not lie down in the dirt that men force on it.'

Eneas isn't an articulate man as the world sees it, but like all the characters in the book he has his own eloquence. Sweetly reproached by his pappy for his poor performance as a correspondent, he replies wryly: 'The writing hand is a rusty hand, that's true.' There are times when Barry misses blarney by only a leprechaun's whisker – when it occurs to Eneas that his pappy is 'a bit of a fool, a bit of a colossal fool' – but there's no doubt that the book is a stylistic triumph. And yet the truth is that the infinite distinction of the writing becomes limitation, almost, since the primal delight adheres to the separate sentences rather than the story they carry. The urge to read on is not really a desire to know what happens to the hero next, but to see what new marvels of phrasing Barry will breed from his stock of pet words.

Eneas's character is distinctly idealised, suffering and bewildered but exempted from serious internal tensions. He meets hatred with weariness but without embitterment. He is less an exile than an involuntary citizen of the world. He suffers mightily, but the prose in which his days and doings are suspended is balm for the reader if not for him. Readers of the book, gratified, selfish, may wish its hero well in a dim sort of way, but would happily see Eneas driven to the top of the barest crag, if that would guarantee his being struck a few thousand more times by the loving lightning of his maker's language.
Observer, 15 March 1998

The structure of this is classic. It opens by jumping forward with the visceral *feel* of the book (while deftly telling, or reminding, readers who the author is), then steps back to provide an outline of the plot and to hint at the themes. This is followed by the bulk of the assessment, helpfully illustrated with quotations. It makes both negative and positive points, but ends on the one that Mars-Jones thinks most important (with which he also opened the review): that the novel's language is beautiful.

His own language is precise and vivid, too. Look, for instance, at that final sentence. And notice how, as an *Observer* writer, he compliments his readers by assuming they have heard of the wandering Trojan hero Aeneas and will recognise the quotation about the relationship of war to diplomacy that he echoes in 'If Barry's prose is poetry carried on by other means . . .'. Most important, though, is that the review provides such a potent *sense* of the novel that readers will know very well, by the end, whether or not they want to read it.

Sylvia Patterson on Tori Amos's album *From the Choirgirl Hotel* in *Frank*:

She is 34 and still believes in fairies. She was raped at gunpoint and still believes in love. She is Tori Amos, 'bonkers banshee piano woman', purveyor of lyrical paeans to the joys of giving God a blow job, and a multi-million-selling 'cult' artiste with the sort of fame which spawns devoted 'fans' who hide in bushes with guns. Thus, as with all extremists, many people (especially boys) cannot be doing with Tori Amos, for she is a wailing siren who sings about blood clots running down your inner thighs – but, of course, these males are crybaby saps who are terrified of women's (sometimes literal) innards.

This time, however, after the chilling 1996 *Boys for Pele* (which signalled 'a change in my relationship with men for good'), she comes to us a glittery-eyed newly wed. But don't be looking for 'love-is-a-many-splendoured-thing' here. She is also a soul-shattered mother-to-be who miscarried her baby in 1997. *From the Choirgirl Hotel* is the story of how she coped and how she didn't and how, in the end, she found a brand-new passion for Life. And how, while she was at it, she found herself a band of musicianly gifted snooksters with whom she expanded her spiky piano dramatics into whole new dimensions of soundscape terror and epic gorgeousness. Which, at least once (on the baying *Cruel*), has turned her into Patti Smith guesting on a particularly 'dark' Tricky song.

This is Amos's shock-free album, featuring no artwork treats like piglets being suckled on her breast (as she did inside *Boys for Pele*); on this sleeve she floats in blackness, with her hands engaged in some flaky-fingered Ted Rogers '321' impersonation (but more likely the magic signalling of Inca binary charms, or some such). So, she's free, and, in freedom, brings us her version of the ubiquitous late-90s epic with a different kind of lyric: 'She's addicted to nicotine patches' goes the hairy *Spark*; 'She's afraid of a light in the dark . . . but she couldn't keep baby alive.' And in *Playboy Mommy* she sings to the spirit of what she was sure was going to be her daughter: 'Don't judge me so harsh little girl . . . you gotta playboy mommy.'

It's sorrow set, however, to some of the most beautiful sounds Amos has ever conjured from her kaleidoscopic mind: the rousing *Raspberry Swirl*, the mournful loveliness of *Liquid Diamonds*, the frankly hysterical *She's Your Cocaine* and the goose-bump caper of *Northern Lad* which breaks your heart in 47 places and then makes you want to leap naked off the top of an Icelandic volcano brimful of finest Viking vodka.

Her voice, too, has found a new fandango to dance. The vocal gymnastics of *Hotel* are berserk to behold, before she coos, 'I'm

still alive . . . I'm still alive . . . I'm still alive.' Tori Amos is, in actual fact, one of those rare people who is Truly Alive; positively exploding, in fact, with life. It is this which makes her 'mad', which is to say she has a personality, big ideas, a bigger heart, and a wise head and something to say about rock'n'roll and pain and sacrifice and joy. *From the Choirgirl Hotel* is the first Tori Amos album you can dance to (on the right kind of drugs). You could even have sex to it and not feel squiffy afterwards. It is more P J Harvey and Portishead than Kate Bush, and the furthest away from the 'mad-woman-with-a-piano' stereotype she has ever been; it's over the lone-piano wall into the multi-layered atmospheric pool of Joni Mitchell and the technology of Massive Attack. And, like all the best ideas, you wonder why she didn't think of it before.
Frank, June 1998

Although this is very different in voice from Adam Mars-Jones's review above, it shares with it the power to make readers experience what the reviewer experienced, to feel the reviewer's enthusiasm and to know, by the end, whether or not the work of art is their kind of thing. This review opens by talking, at length, about the artist: not only because the facts of her life are attention-grabbing but because the album is, in effect, a chapter of her autobiography. The assessment component which follows is apparently nothing but positive, but the odd tongue-in-cheek phrase – 'more likely the magic signalling of Inca binary charms, or some such' – concedes that the album might sometimes veer towards pretentious-ness.

Patterson's language is sometimes more inventive than correct – 'musicianly gifted snooksters' – but never incomprehensible. And although she does, at one point, describe Amos's 'sounds' as 'beautiful', she immediately specifies what she means: 'the goose-bump caper of *Northern Lad* which breaks your heart in 47 places . . . '. (The side-swipes at 'boys' and 'crybaby' men in the opening paragraph are there at least in part because *Frank* is a magazine aimed at women.)

5
Writing online
Tim Holmes

First the good news. Everything you have read so far in this book is entirely relevant for writing online. Now the bad news. Much of what you have read could be completely irrelevant.

A paradox – but one that can be resolved.

To start with the first proposition, good writing is good writing wherever and however it is published. Journalism relies on a few basics for its quality – good story selection, sound research, compelling storytelling and a readable style. The late Nicholas Tomalin's much-quoted answer to a question about the characteristics a journalist needs – 'a plausible manner, rat-like cunning and a little literary ability' – is not the whole truth but encapsulates enough truth to be useful.

But, and here we can start to resolve the paradox, a cunning journalist should be able to write stories differently for different outlets, and the digital platform is nothing if not different. A carefully researched, well-structured 2,000-word feature may sit happily in a printed newspaper or magazine but on a typical computer screen it will go 'below the fold' (that is to say, it will spill off the screen) many times over, so the reader will either be scrolling down constantly or, if the feature is split over a number of pages, clicking onward, ever onward. There are some people, the editor of *Newsweek* among them,[1] who believe that people will not read more than 500 words in one go online – although commonsense and personal experience suggest that anyone really interested in a topic will read for as long as it takes: back to good storytelling. Nevertheless, neither excessive scrolling nor clicking is regarded as desirable in terms of design or usability.

'Usability' is used to measure and describe the ease with which a reader can engage with a website or a page on a website. In print this has been developed over centuries as typefaces, graphics, print technology, the principles of layout and even the look and feel of paper (haptics) have evolved to aid easy reading. Newspaper and magazine design follow well-established rules, or else break them for a particular purpose, and those rules affect the ways in which copy appears on the page. In the online world, the principles of usability for what might be called communication sites have been championed most notably by Jakob Nielsen whose useit.com website contains a wealth of material for writers as well as designers.

At its most basic, usability on a journalism site comes down to efficiency of use – a term which can be unpacked to reveal ease of reading, clear navigation and the ability to complete the intended task simply and without encountering or making any errors. To go back to our hypothetical 2,000-word feature, 'usability' might well mean not having to keep scrolling down or clicking to new screens.

The next question should really be 'how to achieve usability in writing?' but a great many journalism sites have not yet started to put this concept at the heart of their online newspapers or magazines. At present, journalism online can be categorised into three types of writing – shovelware, modified shovelware and net-native.

SHOVELWARE

Shovelware is the rather derogatory term used for material originally written for one medium that is then 'shovelled' straight into a different medium or format without modification or consideration of appearance or usability. It was first used to describe cheaply compiled CD-ROMs of games or software, then to describe games designed for one platform that were adapted to a different platform with no attempt to cater for the new platform's capabilities or restrictions. In time it came to be applied to journalistic copy written for print and shovelled straight onto a webpage. It has also been applied to television shows created for conventional broadcast but now being shovelled onto mobile phones.

Technically, shovelware is as easy to execute as any other computer-based cut-and-paste operation and although it is clearly efficient in terms of time and resources it ignores usability and is generally given low status as a job and a product: members of the production teams whose job it is to dump a paper's content online are often referred to as web monkeys.

However, I would argue that most print-based sites, newspapers and magazines, have moved away from basic shovelware and now offer what might be called modified shovelware.

MODIFIED SHOVELWARE

The *Guardian* is widely recognised in the UK as a newspaper that has wholeheartedly embraced the online world through its Guardian-Unlimited website. Click onto it, however, and you will find a great deal of the content simply reproduces the news reports and features that appear in the printed newspaper – shovelware. On the other hand, the copy is framed by extra material that could only appear online: there are hyperlinks to related stories, features or extra material like podcasts, graphics and maps, tools for RSS (Really Simple Syndication) and mobile feeds, clickable advertisements and a facility for readers to comment on individual stories. All of this is presented within an easily navigated site that constantly invites readers to participate in the communication process through the Comment Is Free section.

This model has also been adopted by other newspapers such as the *Daily Telegraph*, which moved its editorial offices to a new site specifically designed to facilitate this new mode of publishing. There have been high-profile casualties among the senior editorial staff, most of which are (anecdotally at least) attributed to their unwillingness to submit to the demands of so-called 360-degree publishing. The new regime encompasses not only the now routine podcasts but also TelegraphTV: click onto the Telegraph.co.uk site and right at the top of the page you are offered a video of the latest story – a video to which formerly print-only newspaper journalists are expected to contribute.

Periodical journalists cannot escape from these developments either because, to take one example, the same principle can be found at *Stuff*, a print magazine which focuses on technological gadgets and girls, also an online site (stuffmagazine.com) which offers videos, lists and links to Maxim radio – and now an internet TV station (stuff.tv) on which you can see the magazine staff (most of whom will have been recruited as print journalists) reviewing kit or get 360-degree slideshows of gadgets. *Stuff* is published by Dennis Publishing, which launched *Monkey* magazine in 2006 as an online-only weekly for young men.

This, however, is straying from modified shovelware because whereas stuffmagazine.com qualifies for that category, stuff.tv has no direct print equivalent and *Monkey* has no print analogue at all.

As well as the framing or context, as on GuardianUnlimited, modified shovelware can also encompass shortened or otherwise amended pieces originally written for print. Such material may be augmented with 'rich' additions like comments, related blogs and suggested links to other stories, videos and podcasts. In these instances the writer, subeditor or page editor will have been given a word count and a brief for the extras and there should be no great technical or technological secrets to doing the job.

The digitally reproduced copies of newspapers and magazines available online also fit into this category. These editions are produced using specialised software developed by Ceros or Olivetree or in the widely available Adobe PDF format (which works pretty seamlessly with Adobe's InDesign page layout software). Once downloaded, digital editions can be read just like a print version – the pages 'turn' and the print layout is reproduced exactly, pictures and all. Clearly, as far as the writer is concerned there are no special considerations here at all and in one respect digital editions might be categorised as plain old shovelware on a grand scale since they simply replicate the entire content in its original layout. However, they may also incorporate the ability to search, to clip outtakes and to embed video or other 'rich' additions, as well as being able to return statistical information on the number and origins of views to the publisher.

NET-NATIVE COMPOSITION

So far, the first part of my opening paradox has applied: with shovelware and modified shovelware everything in this book about writing for journalists applies, because there is no difference in practice. If you are writing for a print newspaper or magazine and that writing will be applied, wholesale, to a different platform, your reportage or features should follow the principles laid out in the other chapters.

But when we consider the third category of online journalism, net-native composition, the other part of the paradox applies: much of what you have read could be completely irrelevant.

Net-native material differs from shovelware and modified shovelware in being intended for online use right from the start, and this is where the writer has to learn a number of new tricks: some are simple matters of tone and vocabulary; others are more technically demanding and will require new practical skills. Net-native material naturally incorporates pictures, hyperlinks, audio and video, sometimes harvested from non-professional sources but often provided by the writer. The intention is to provide depth and richness of texture rather than simply extensive verbiage, so that instead of a 5,000-word feature that has to be read off a screen (or printed out) web users are presented with a multimedia package from which they can choose to read text, link to another page for more background, run audio or video that adds information and authenticity, add a comment to the debate among readers, start a blog or add to their own blog, register the page or story with digg, del.icio.us, newsvine or any one of the increasing number of community/social/aggregation sites.

Much of this, as you will have grasped, will require you to operate hardware and manipulate software. There is no way around this and nostalgia for an older, simpler, time when an ace reporter could phone through copy before retiring to the pub and waiting for the print to appear without even touching a typewriter is best left to the pages of Michael Frayn's wonderful novel *Towards the End of the Morning* (1967). As the book in your hands is not concerned with software instruction, it is not the right place to run through technical how-tos and, in any case, such content would be pointless. The thing about new media, to apply a generic name, is that it is always new and the industry standard of today might be different tomorrow.

Take the page layout software QuarkXPress as an example. Ten years ago no one could foresee Quark being usurped as the programme of choice for magazines and newspapers: it had a huge installed base and there was an equally large amount of skill-capital tied up in it. A decade later Adobe InDesign has made massive inroads. Similarly with webpage software. Five years ago I would have recommended a modern journalist to have at least a working knowledge of DreamWeaver, plus some basic HTML. Now, the HTML might still be useful but most journalists will be feeding their stories into a skinned content management system rather than individually tailored pages.

Where does this leave us with writing for online outlets? Nowhere much, and it is important to grasp that there is not yet any standard advice or a set of basic rules to apply, at least not as far as execution is concerned. The sites or sources which offer advice about writing online not only repeat each other, they essentially repeat what you will find in Chapter 2 of this book, 'Writing news', only not so succinctly and without examples. (There are some exceptions to this listed at the end of the chapter.)

If nothing else, this shows that the foundations of journalism are still entirely relevant – locating stories which will interest or be of use to your readers, researching those stories using a variety of sources, finding the right people to interview and interviewing them effectively, knowing what official material you are entitled to, checking at all stages for accuracy. The journalist is both an aggregator and a filter of information and must have the ability to order that information into a considered narrative.

However, 'considered narrative' does not always mean a story with a beginning, a middle and an end, in that order. Unlike print publications, a digital magazine or newspaper does not necessarily focus on reading. As *Monkey* magazine's publicity material declares, 'You can watch videos and movie trailers, listen to the latest in music and share incredible stuff with your friends.'[2]

'Feature articles thrive in a print environment,' writes Ari Rosenberg in an article for *Online Publishing Insider*. 'They don't translate well online. If online users wanted to engage with full-length, feature-sized articles, they would read a magazine. Instead, they come to websites with the intention to spend as little time as possible to get what they came for. Content offered online needs to fit inside these shorter attention spans.'[3]

In technical terms, print favours linear composition whereas online is naturally a non-linear medium. Allan Kotmel of Rensselaer Polytechnic Institute, New York, explains the difference thus:

> Linear writing is *straight-line* writing. Most papertext documents are linear. A linear document would have a fairly definite beginning, middle and ending. Most arguments are structured linearly with an introduction, supporting information, and a conclusion. Non-linear writing is more associative. Non-linear writing involves many different paths. . . . There may or may not be a beginning, but there is rarely a definite path or a single ending. This makes for a more reader-based document, and allows the reader to make choices.[4]

If you want to get even more theoretical, the French philosopher/literary critic Roland Barthes came up with a concept that covers exactly this situation. He posited that texts could be classified as 'readerly' or 'writerly'. The former denotes a linear narrative that has a fixed, predetermined meaning, leaving the reader as a mere receiver of information. The writerly text contains a proliferation of meanings and the reader takes a creative role in constructing the meaning. In the book *S/Z* Barthes's description of the writerly makes it sound very like a website. It is:

> a galaxy of signifiers, not a structure of signifieds; it has no
> beginning; it is reversible; we gain access to it by several entrances,
> none of which can be authoritatively declared to be the main one;
> the codes it mobilizes extend as far as the eye can reach, they are
> indeterminable.[5]

In the world of net-native writing, 'writerly' takes on a new meaning,
for although conventional story sources are still relevant and necessary,
there is a massive new resource that must be taken into account – non-
professional sources, or what media commentator Paul Bradshaw (also a
philosopher, in effect) calls 'accidental journalists'. This term can be used
to signify the range of what is often categorised as user-generated content
and citizen journalism. There have been several well-known instances of
non-professional material leading news coverage over the past few years
– the Buncefield oil depot explosion and the 7/7 bombings in the London
Underground are just two examples where camera phone images far from
normal broadcast quality were heavily drawn on.

There are even grounds to argue that as far as online journalism is concerned, the 'journalist' has to relinquish control because participation
matters more than quality. Clay Shirky certainly follows that line of
thought:

> Media people often criticize the content on the internet for being
> unedited, because everywhere one looks, there is low quality – bad
> writing, ugly images, poor design. What they fail to understand
> is that the internet is strongly edited, but the editorial judgment is
> applied at the edges, not the center, and it is applied after the fact,
> not in advance.[6]

That is to say, if it's bad, people won't link to it and if they don't link to
it, it will sink down the search engine results; if it's bad, people won't
want to share it or rate it on Slashdot, digg, del.icio.us or newsvine, and
this becomes a very practical and effective way of raising the quality of
what gets read, without needing to control what gets written.

Simon Caulkin, management editor of the *Observer*, made a similar point
about open source software like Firefox, Linux or the 'apps' for FaceBook.
They are developed by volunteers and 'they use peer review by many
rather than control of the few, the intrinsic motivation of work rather
than monetary reward, self-selection rather than fiat for resource allo-
cation, and perpetual, continuous improvement'.[7]

Pertinently, another part of Caulkin's piece notes it is important to
recognise that 'human beings weren't born to be employees' if new
management techniques suitable for the age of the internet are to be

developed. This is just as applicable for the modern journalist: the non-professional accidental journalist and the community of communication are not employees and you have to find ways of working with them to everyone's advantage. And if you, as a professional journalist, have to make yourself open to incorporating the contributions of accidental journalists, there is yet another side to the bargain when it comes to making your work 'writerly' – let go of it and suspend your professional criticism.

> 'Content has a life outside the brand,' Debbie Djordjevic, editorial director of Hearst Digital, told the PPA Magazines Business Media Conference in May 2007. Magazines need to be in contact with their readers on a daily basis and this means experimentation in blogging, video and pod casting – experiments that don't need to be pitch perfect.

> 'You need to take on board that it can afford to be rough around the edges rather than beautifully crafted, because sometimes beautifully crafted and finished lacks pace and excitement,' said Djordjevic.[8]

And if you really want to see what 'rough around the edges' looks like, dial up whateverlife.com. The pink splodge that will fill your screen was, in September 2006, the third most popular site among teenagers in the USA, according to Nielsen/NetRatings.[9] Without further research we can only speculate why, but Nielsen noted that the site offers tools for customising social networking sites like MySpace and Bebo, and, more importantly for this chapter, in November 2006 the site's founder (17-year-old Ashley Qualls, who set it up when she was 14) launched a magazine sub-site based entirely on what the site-users provided. This is similar to what iVillage.com claims to do, but iVillage has long had a professional structure to turn users' ideas into readable content. Whateverlife magazine flared for a while but had gone rather quiet at the time of writing. Nevertheless, it has lasted longer than *Jellyfish*, the cool, slick, highly professional online launch from NatMags that was intended to bolster *CosmoGIRL* but disappeared shortly after the demise of the print magazine in August 2007. 'The 20-week trial period has been extremely valuable', said NatMags MD Duncan Edwards, 'but we could not see a sustainable business model emerging': whateverlife.com probably has no business model but it is still there, working.

So if anyone from a commuter with a cameraphone to a 14-year-old web geek can do it, we may be driven to ask – what is journalism? At its simplest it is finding things out and telling people about them. And the thing that defines professional journalism may lie more in the first of those functions than in the second. Whatever craft secrets we think we possess, however well we can turn a phrase or contrive a cunningly punning headline, in the machine-mediated world of online communication, the two things that will bring your work to public attention are clear labelling and the use of key words that search engines can identify, and content that is useful to the community you target.

Most online readers will not reach your work, if they reach it at all, through the front door. Most online readers will not call up the splash-page of your magazine or newspaper and then work their way through until they come across your gem of a piece – they are far more likely to come straight at it from the results thrown up by a search engine query.

This has led to a new science of search-engine optimisation, which can be summarised as key words, short words, old words. Winston Churchill recognised their value: 'short words are best and the old words when short are best of all'. This is quoted in the *Economist*'s style guide, but if you feel it curbs your creativity consider the following. When the *Daily Mail* was launched in 1895 it was dismissed by Lord Salisbury as being 'written for clerks by clerks' because the short, punchy journalism of the 'Northcliffe revolution' was far removed from the ponderous prose of the politico-philosophical periodicals (the 'reviews') in which Salisbury and his class pontificated. Yet with the benefit of hindsight we can see the new style of journalism led directly to the clever headlines of the *Sun* in its heyday; with hindsight we can see that Alfred Harmsworth's demands for shorter, brighter, tighter writing were actually a spur to creativity rather than a restriction. The same will almost certainly be true for online writing.

If you are still not satisfied that your writing skills can be fully exercised then go away and write a book like, say, *In Cold Blood*. Or if you're not quite up to that, Sebastian Junger's *The Perfect Storm* is a wonderful mix of fact and imagination. Failing that, you should be able to reproduce the success of *Longitude* by Dava Sobel because that started life as a magazine feature. Long form journalism seems to have found a happy home in the book trade, as a glance at any non-fiction bestseller list of recent years will confirm.

But even if 'writing' becomes less valued in online journalism, 'finding things out' perhaps becomes of greater importance as a mark of profes-sionalism. Not just finding things out, of course, but making sure that what you find out stands up to scrutiny, that it is as close as you can get to a true record of the facts. The sources you use to achieve this expand exponentially online: the letter, email or phone call tipping you off to a good story merge into the forums created around your publication (it does have reader forums, doesn't it?), into the comments on the blog entries you post (you do keep a blog, don't you?), into the databases of information which can be mined for trends or merged with other databases to create a third entity – an entity that may eventually be created by the readers themselves.

This is not the place to give detailed instruction in data mining, but it is worth pointing out that such journalism has a long history. Philip Meyer wrote *Precision Journalism: A Reporter's Guide to Social Science Methods* in 1973 and everything that has happened since has not only made his ideas more relevant, it has made it possible to add all sorts of other tools. If you want a taste of what can be achieved, look at www.chicagocrime.org, which combines Chicago police department data with geographical data from Google Maps that pinpoints each incident on a street map (or satellite image). For more ideas, the site founder's blog can be found at www.holovaty.com. Alternatively, tips on this and other useful areas can be found in *Journalism 2.0: How to Survive and Thrive*, which can be downloaded for free from the Knight Citizen News Network.

But – to return to the theme of professionalism – journalism is not the same as raw data or material acquired 'accidentally'. As Lucas Graves noted in *Wired* magazine:

> Yammering about a story you read in the *New York Times* doesn't qualify as reporting, even when it's 'participatory' yammering. But news – ie, real, original information – is news whether it breaks on NBC or your sister's boy-band site.

No matter how compelling the still or moving image, no matter how affecting the verbal account, that material, that 'news', must be set into a considered narrative, must be given a context and an explanation.

And major stories require major resources if they are to be covered fully or investigated properly. Graves adds:

> The pros still have one thing most amateurs don't: resources. Grassroots reporting fills the gaps in mainstream coverage, keeps members of the old guard on their toes, and shines when there's a premium on fast facts from the scene. But laypeople can't do much with a story like Watergate or Enron. 'Big investigative projects require deep pockets,' [Dan] Gillmor says. 'I'm not trying to tell anyone that we don't need paid journalists. I hope for an eco-system where many forms of information can survive and thrive.'[10]

Many media commentators and journalism educators have theorised about what such ecosystems might look like and in one of the most compelling Paul Bradshaw takes that old staple of the geometry of journalism, the inverted triangle, and doubles it into a diamond. To summarise, he follows the newsgathering and dissemination process through from initial alert to blog-quality first draft to more polished article or package, into contextualisation by hyperlinking to background material, reflection or analysis, interactive exchanges with and between the producers and consumers, ending up in what Bradshaw calls customisation – anything from an RSS feed to a drillable (and thus mashable) database. See http://www.onlinejournalismblog.com/2007/09/17/a-model-for-the-21st-century-newsroom-pt1-the-news-diamond/ for the full article, complete with diagram and a link to the second part, which proposes a model for distributed journalism. Here's a brief taster of the latter: 'the modern journalist's role needs to move above the content'.

This seems like a good point to return to TelegraphTV and stuff.tv, both of which have recognisable content and recognisable journalists providing it. But does it mean that we must all become television journalists?

I believe not, and I can draw a useful analogy with my print journalism experience to illustrate why. I spent much of my career in journalism working on motorcycle magazines and during that time I was under no illusion about my abilities as a rider; I knew for a fact that many of our readers were faster or more skilled, just as I knew that many had deeper technical knowledge. So what gave me the right to occupy my position on a specialist title? The fact was, I got pretty good at finding or contriving stories which appealed to the readers, I could tell those stories well, and I was able to contribute to that feeling of belonging to a club characteristic of successful magazines. I knew, or could find out, what questions needed to be asked and if I didn't know the answers myself I could locate someone with the necessary knowledge.

It's the same with non-linear journalism, as Tom Dunmore, *Stuff*'s editor, explained to the 2007 PPA Magazines and Business Media Conference:

> Clearly making a video is very intensive on your resources – it takes a day of my week. It's also relatively expensive to produce, especially as you need to get location, cameraman, editing. We've kept the cost pretty low, but it is a significant investment.
>
> Most journalists know how to write but very few know how to stand in front of a camera. You can multitask, but people need to get confident in order to do it. It's worth spending time getting the attitude and tone right, because video can bring so much of that to site. You can't just put a camera in someone's hand and expect them to produce content.[11]

So what can you usefully learn to help you develop as an online writer? The following list is neither comprehensive nor necessarily, for obvious reasons, up to date, but it does give a snapshot of some useful skills. Software mentioned by name should be assumed to carry the suffix 'or current equivalent'.

YOUR BRAIN

This is the obvious place to start. It is no longer enough to think of news stories in the inverted pyramid, punchy intro, telling-and-retelling structure, or features as an elegant Doric column of intro, bridge, body and outro. In journalism, online 'stories' become combinations of text, sound, vision, movement and stillness. There are tools that enable you to combine these elements in many ways and it is up to you to find out what works. There are suggestions for further reading – and self-education – at the end of this chapter.

BLOGGING

Even if the other suggestions in this section leave you unconvinced, keeping a blog has almost become a necessity for a journalist: indeed, some editors have declared that they would not hire a journalist who did not have one. Technically it is simple – if you can use Word, you can set up and maintain a blog.

A blog can help a journalist in many ways: it adds the ability to publish information outside the normal production cycle and story format; it may allow the establishment of a deeper relationship with the community of readers; it can act like an outliner, a way to compile notes or organise story strands, or an aggregator of useful links; and if you find the right tone and persona it can add to your personal brand by combining authority with personality (as *Journalism 2.0* puts it).

Entries should be tightly written but not hackneyed, to the point but not terse, conversational in tone and linked to other sites and articles (the link is also an attribution). Experiment with adding audio and video as you see fit. Top your entries with a headline that search engines will find, tail them with as many tags as are relevant and 'claim' your blog on Technorati and everywhere else you can. When other people find you, as they will if you keep it up and keep on message, it can be both satisfying and, if a conversation starts, illuminating.

RSS FEEDS

This is related to Your Brain, because you will naturally want, and need, to keep up with developments in the media and communications industries, and if you just bookmark all those useful sites you come across you can bet they will rest peacefully in the bookmarks folder, undisturbed for months at a time.

The answer is to use an RSS reader/aggregator. This allows you to subscribe to RSS feeds that will constantly update news from the sources you think are useful. There are several types and flavours of reader – I have found Netvibes (free from www.netvibes.com) simple, reliable and fun. Once you are a registered user you can access your pages and feeds from any webbed-up computer, anywhere.

You can, of course, also use this technology to keep up with the news from your area of speciality, beat or patch.

FLASH

A good many people will associate Flash with irritating animated introduction pages that, fortunately, usually have a 'skip intro' option. It can, however, be used to create stories that incorporate text, images, movies and sounds, allowing the journalist to draw on a range of storytelling tools. As just one example, take sports reporting. In a printed newspaper or magazine, phases of play in games like football or rugby are shown in static graphics using lines and arrows, which convey little or no sense of movement; broadcast footage may only focus on a few players or one angle. Using Flash, it is possible to create a moving graphic that depicts the interaction between players and allows the reader to get a better overview of who did what when. Agence France-Presse produces a Flash package for the Tour de France every year and you can see the 2004 version (and other stories) on Mindy McAdams's Flashjournalism.com site by calling up http://www.flashjournalism.com/examples/en/index.html.

This principle can be applied to many types of story, and can be used to explain temporal, historical and even political relationships. One of the most effective Flash stories I have seen was created by a student at a Spanish journalism college; it explained and contextualised the attempted takeover of parliament in 1981 by Lt-Col. Antonio Tejero Molino, making use of customised graphics, extracts from contemporary newspapers, still photographs and linking text. In a few minutes it told me what it would have taken several pages of a printed account to convey.

One drawback of Flash is that not all computers will be running it, so not everyone will be able to see material created with it.

PHOTOSHOP

Photoshop has gained an unfortunate association with stunts such as the one in which the then culture minister, James Purnell, became involved, appearing in a 'photograph' of an event he did not even attend. Of course, photographs have been manipulated for decades, as demonstrated by the famous example of Trotsky being removed from a photograph that originally showed him and Lenin together in Red Square on the second anniversary of the Russian Revolution (1919).

But Photoshop – indeed, any fully featured image-processing software – can do much more than crop, scale and add or subtract personnel, useful though those functions are. You can clean up old images, pull out details of particular interest and create complex, multi-layered graphics.

At the very least a journalist working in the digital world should know how to resize images and save them in the correct format for the job in hand.

GOOGLE MASHUPS

Mashup is a new, and useful, word which denotes the process of combining two formerly separate sets of data. In music it is applied to artefacts such as the *Grey Album* (2004) produced by Danger Mouse – a merging of *The White Album* by the Beatles (1968) and Jay-Z's *Black Album* (2003). In journalism one of the best-known mashups is Adrian Holovaty's chicagocrime.org, mentioned above. Anyone can merge a Google map with other data to create a storytelling, interactive graphic and it is not hard to think of possibilities for augmenting – or creating – stories in outdoor or hiking magazines, motoring and motorcycling titles, charting the appearance of giant carp or exotic predators for fishing magazines. All it needs is imagination and experimentation combined with a willingness to convert the 'writing' into a database of searchable fields.

I-MOVIE

The movie editing software included free with every new Apple computer is so easy to use that a complete novice can put together a passable production within an hour of first firing up the package – there is a very good step-by-step tutorial in the Help menu. DV cameras are relatively cheap and simple but it still helps to have good raw footage to work with, so a bit of tuition or self-tuition in shooting video is advisable; various sites are suggested at the end of this chapter.

AUDACITY

This is free, open-source, award-winning software that lets you record and edit sounds. To do this it is also necessary to invest in an audio recorder, but most journalists use them anyway. There are many inexpensive models available; just make sure that the one you buy has the means to upload files. As *Journalism* 2.0 has it:

> You might be tempted to buy a $50 version because, hey, it says it's a digital recorder. But unless you can transfer the files from the recorder to your computer, you will be unable to get the files onto a Web site where readers can listen to them. So it would be like writing a story on a computer and not being able to send it to your editor.

Finally, and although I almost promised I would not do this, some general tips for online writing.

- *Keep it simple.* Your readers will come from all over the world, so demotic slang or opaque phraseology is not appropriate. This applies to body copy and page furniture.
- *Include key words.* Horribly reductionist though it may be, your online work will stand or fall on whether it can be found by search engines. This means that you must remember to include the actual, simple words that classify your piece.
- That's it.

And if you don't believe anything I have written above, here's a useful list from Mindy McAdams. Journalism students may find it encouraging and older hands may find it discouraging. In a classic illustration of feature writing theory we have circled back to that paradox again.

- A new skills set is demanded for the best jobs and for leadership positions.
- The days of five clips getting a student a good job are over at major media outlets.
- The best jobs out there require a strong knowledge of journalism and technology.
- A digital portfolio will become commonplace.
- Students who can shoot photos, video, collect audio, edit and post to the web will have employers knocking on their door.
- Students must have a better sense of the economics and business of media.
- Media must embrace the computer science/engineering and business disciplines.
- Every student should be a serious blogger.
- The pace of change is quickening.
- New media is not a fad, but a fact.
- Entrepreneurship in media is needed desperately.
- Marketing, advertising and PR are way ahead of journalism in adopting innovation.

FURTHER BROWSING

Bloggers (most have links to dozens of other blogs)

Paul Bradshaw – http://onlinejournalismblog.com/
Mindy McAdams – http://mindymcadams.com/tojou/
Adrian Holovaty – http://www.holovaty.com/
Paul Conley – http://paulconley.blogspot.com/
Clay Shirky – http://www.shirky.com/

Storytelling resources

Audacity – http://audacity.sourceforge.net/
Drupal content management systems – http://drupal.org/
Technorati – http://technorati.com/
Bloglines RSS – http://www.bloglines.com/
Soundslides – http://www.soundslides.com/
Netvibes – http://www.netvibes.com
Blog platforms – http://wordpress.com/, http://www.blogger.com, http://www.ning.com/

Learning and research

Journalism 2.0 – http://www.j-lab.org/Journalism_20.pdf
Googlemaps how-to – http://googlemapsapi.blogspot.com/2007/04/
   introducing-3-maps-apikml-tutorials-in.html
Community journalism – http://j-learning.org/
Online journalism – http://www.cyberjournalist.net/
Online news – http://www.journalists.org/
The Poynter Institute – http://www.poynter.org/
Shooting video – http://newsvideographer.com/
News University – http://www.newsu.org/
Jakob Nielsen – http://www.useit.com/
The Bivings Group – http://www.bivings.com/
USA Today's guide to interactive storytelling – http://www.usatoday.
   com/test/bag-of-tricks/index.html

Multimedia articles and features

Find the right candidate
http://www.usatoday.com/news/politics/election2008/candidate-match-
   game.htm

Tour de France 2007
http://www.nytimes.com/packages/flash/sports/tdf2007/

Compare sprinters
http://www.nytimes.com/2007/06/01/sports/playmagazine/20070602_SP
   RINTER_GRAPHIC.html?_r=1&oref=slogin

Accident black spots
http://www.madison.com/wsj/projects/devils/index.html

The Darfur crisis
http://www.washingtonpost.com/wp-srv/world/interactives/chad/index.
   html

World Heritage Sites
http://www.world-heritage-tour.org

World statistics in graphic form
http://www.gapminder.org

Other sites

Whateverlife – http://whateverlife.com
Monkey magazine – http://www.monkeymag.co.uk
Monkeyslum – http://www.monkeyslum.com/
Mykindaplace – http://www.mykindaplace.com/hi.aspx
Thisisamagazine – http://www.thisisamagazine.com

NOTES

1 <http://mrmagazine.wordpress.com/2007/05/01/god-and-war-newsweeks-meacham-favorite-things-and-other-words-of-wisdom/>
2 <http://www.monkeymag.co.uk/registration>
3 <http://blogs.mediapost.com/online_publishing_insider/?p=88>
4 <http://www.rpi.edu/dept/llc/webclass/web/filigree/kotmel/linear.html>
5 Roland Barthes (1974), *S/Z: An Essay* (trans. Richard Miller), New York: Hill and Wang, p. 5.
6 <http://www.shirky.com/writings/broadcast_and_community.html>
7 Simon Caulkin (2007) 'Internet could put the boss class out of a job', *Observer* Business section, 14 September 2007, p. 10.
8 <http://www.pressgazette.co.uk/story.asp?storycode=37752>
9 <http://www.Nielsen-netratings.com/pr/pr_061011.pdf>
10 <www.wired.com/wircd/archive/13.09/start.html?pg=2>
11 <http://www.pressgazette.co.uk/story.asp?storycode=37752>

6
Style

MURDER YOUR DARLINGS

The traditional view on English style is simply put. Be clear; avoid orna-
ment; let the message reveal itself. From Samuel Johnson and Jonathan
Swift in the eighteenth century to George Orwell in the twentieth
and Elmore Leonard in the twenty-first, writers and literary critics have
agreed. Style is not something to be strained for or added on: it is there in
the writer – or the subject – waiting to be expressed. What is needed is
plainness, decorum, economy, precision – above all, clarity. What is not
needed is rhetoric or embellishment.

Quoting a college tutor, Dr Johnson pronounced: 'Read over your com-
positions, and where ever you meet with a passage which you think
is particularly fine, strike it out.' And echoing Dr Johnson, Sir Arthur
Quiller-Couch told Cambridge undergraduates in 1913: 'Whenever you
feel an impulse to perpetrate a piece of exceptionally fine writing, obey it
– whole-heartedly – and delete it before sending your manuscript to press.
Murder your darlings.'

As his Oxford opposite number, J Middleton Murry, noted a few years
later, 'These *obiter dicta* of the masters . . . all point the same way; they
all lay stress solely on the immediate nature of style; they all reduce the
element of art or artifice to nothingness.'

A famous campaigner for simple English, Sir Ernest Gowers, wrote an
influential book intended to help civil servants in their use of written
English – he called it *Plain Words*. It is full of passages like

> The most prevalent disease in present-day writing is a tendency
> to say what one has to say in as complicated a way as possible.
> Instead of being simple, terse and direct, it is stilted, long-winded

and circumlocutory; instead of choosing the simple word it prefers the unusual; instead of the plain phrase, the cliché.

In the United States the traditional message has been exactly the same. William Strunk, whose book *The Elements of Style* was later revised by E B White, wrote in 1918:

> Young writers often suppose that style is a garnish for the meat of prose, a sauce by which a dull dish is made palatable. Style has no such separate entity; it is non-detachable, unfilterable. . . . The approach to style is by way of plainness, simplicity, orderliness, sincerity.

More recently, in a piece published in the *New York Times*, the crime writer Elmore Leonard issued his own rules of good writing, such as: 'Never use a verb other than "said" to carry dialogue' and 'Never use an adverb to modify the verb "said"' and 'If it sounds like writing, I rewrite it.'

This emphasis on plainness and simplicity has been repeated by those who lay down the law about journalistic style. *The Economist Style Guide*, first published in the 1980s, quotes George Orwell's 'six elementary rules' from a famous essay, 'Politics and the English Language', written in 1946:

1   Never use a metaphor, simile or other figure of speech which you are used to seeing in print.
2   Never use a long word where a short word will do.
3   If it is possible to cut out a word, always cut it out.
4   Never use the passive where you can use the active.
5   Never use a foreign phrase, a scientific word or a jargon word if you can think of an everyday English equivalent.
6   Break any of these rules sooner than say anything outright barbarous.

THE FOG INDEX

The Americans, who adopted journalism education and training before the British, have developed a systematic way of measuring the readability of newspapers and magazines. The journalism trainer Robert Gunning gave his name in 1944 to the Gunning Fog Index, which sets out to show how clear or obscure ('foggy') writing is. The index is based on counting the long words and working out the length of an average sentence in a sample passage. A formula translates this into the approximate number of years of education needed to understand it. The higher the fog index, the harder the passage is to understand.

Thus a popular American TV magazine scores 6, equivalent to sixth grade or six years of education, while the *Ladies' Home Journal* scores 8, the *National Geographic* 10, and *Time* magazine 12 – equivalent to high school senior or 12 years of education.

Some British trainers apply the index to our media: a typical airport novel would score 6, a downmarket newspaper (the *Mirror*) 8–10, a middle-market paper (the *Express*) 10–12, an upmarket paper (the *Telegraph*) 12–14, a specialist periodical (*Pulse*) 14–16 – and the small print in an insurance company document 20. Whether or not you adopt the index, the idea that underlies it is essential: to write successfully for a publication you must write so that its readers understand you.

WRITE THE WAY YOU TALK

In the orthodox Anglo-American tradition there is a second commandment: that good writing should mirror speech rather than aspire to be something else, something artificial, contrived, self-consciously literary. As William Hazlitt put it in the early nineteenth century:

> To write a genuine familiar or true English style is to write as any-one would speak in common conversation, who had a thorough command and choice of words, or who could discourse with ease, force and perspicuity, setting aside all pedantic and oratorical flourishes.

Later, Cyril Connolly attacked what he called the mandarin style

> loved by literary pundits, by those who would make the written word as unlike as possible to the spoken one. It is the style of those writers whose tendency is to make their language convey more than they mean or more than they feel, it is the style of most artists and all humbugs.

Both Hazlitt and Connolly were journalists – and their message has been enthusiastically endorsed by later experts on journalistic style. Harold Evans in his classic *Newsman's English* (republished in 2000 as *Essential English for Journalists, Editors and Writers*) quotes Connolly with approval and recommends 'a clear, muscular and colloquial style'; Nicholas Bagnall in *Newspaper Language* quotes Hazlitt and calls his 'the best definition I know of the true language of journalism'.

In one of his 10 principles of clear statement Robert Gunning takes the argument a stage further and urges 'Write the way you talk', while John Whale in his book *Put It in Writing* repeats the point in more formal British English – 'Write as you speak.'

For all sorts of reasons – including the powerful influence on print of TV and radio – this link between the spoken word and journalistic writing is now stronger than ever.

METAPHORS ARE MORE FUN

Both these ideas – write plainly and clearly; write as you speak – are obviously relevant to anyone learning journalism. The first is essential in basic news writing and instructional copy (telling readers how to mend a fuse, make an omelette, fill in a tax form). But that is not the end of the matter.

Unfortunately – in journalism as in writing generally – the rule is often assumed to apply across the board, whereas it does not. Good style cannot be reduced to the slogan 'Write plainly and clearly.'

As the American writer Richard Lanham points out in a little-known but forceful attack on the classics, *Style: An Anti-Textbook*: 'People seldom write simply to be clear. They have designs on their fellow men. Pure prose is as rare as pure virtue, and for the same reasons.'

Lanham ridicules The Books for preaching that the best style is the never noticed, for recommending that prose style should, like the state under Marxism, wither away, leaving the plain facts shining unto themselves. 'People, even literary people, seldom content themselves with being clear. They invent jargons, argot . . . and even when they succeed in being clear it is often only to seem clever.'

It is not easy to find examples of great writers who wrote 'plainly and clearly'. Certainly not the poets Chaucer, Shakespeare, Keats and Eliot; and not the novelists from Fielding to Martin Amis by way of Dickens and Lawrence. Even the literary preachers didn't always practise plainness. Dr Johnson was famously florid rather than plain; Swift, the scourge of looseness and incorrectness, often got carried away.

On the other hand, George Orwell, journalist, novelist, literary critic, is perhaps the best exponent of the plain style in English literature. His work is content-driven and in many ways he provides an excellent model of control, simplicity and precision.

Then of course there is Ernest Hemingway, master storyteller, Nobel prizewinner, another novelist who started as a journalist – his style is famous for its apparent simplicity. Here's a paragraph from his last great book, *The Old Man and the Sea*:

> The old man had seen many great fish. He had seen many that weighed more than a thousand pounds and he had caught two of that size in his life, but never alone. Now alone, and out of sight of land, he was fast to the biggest fish that he had ever seen and bigger than he had ever heard of, and his left hand was still as tight as the gripped claws of an eagle.

Note that word 'apparent' applied to 'simplicity': here is the use of deliberate repetition (for example, 'had seen many' repeated early on), the characteristic use of 'and' (three times in the last sentence), the gradual increase in sentence length, all contributing to a rich and powerful rhythm. The paragraph ends with the simile of the eagle's claws – which stands out from the 'plainness' of the rest.

Hemingway's prose then is not as simple as it looks. Other great writers of the twentieth century were dense (Faulkner), ornate (Nabokov) – or just plain difficult (Joyce).

As in literature so in personal life, politics, business, advertising – how can anybody argue that all speakers and writers aspire to clarity first and foremost? Of course, they have to be capable of clarity and know when to use it. But they don't use it all the time, not if they are arguing a case, wooing a woman or a man, playing a scene for laughs, showing off, selling a secondhand car . . .

Then there is the delight that so many speakers and writers take in playing with words. As Lanham puts it:

> People seldom content themselves with plain utterance even in daily life. It gets boring. . . . They prefer the metaphorical, the indirect expression to the straightforward, literal one. They are not trying to be literary. Metaphors are just more fun.

CLARITY, CLARITY, CLARITY*

But there is a strong – indeed overwhelming – argument that, whatever politicians, lovers and secondhand car dealers may do, journalists must be

---

* This heading is in fact a quotation from *The Elements of Style*: it is clear – but the rhetoric of repetition makes it far from plain.

clear above all; that journalism has no point otherwise; that an essential part of its function is to interrogate the politicians and conmen, to represent and communicate with the ordinary person confronted by authority, salesmanship, jargon, pretension . . . Journalism must be clear.

Individual words and phrases must be clear so that your reader can understand them. For example, you must be careful with technical terms – a word suitable for a specialist periodical might be too abstruse for a daily paper. And, just as important, anything you write must be clear in structure: you must say things in the right order – without aimlessly repeating yourself or digressing too far from your main point.

Does this mean that the traditionalists are right after all? For journalism (as opposed to other kinds of writing) do we have to go back to the slogan 'Write plainly and clearly'?

Certainly, if journalism could be reduced to plainness and clarity, life would be much simpler and well-edited listings pages could stand as the perfect model of good style. But obviously this won't do. So we have to think again.

Plainness and clarity are associated for two reasons. First, to repeat the point, there are certain kinds of journalistic writing (basic news, instructional copy) where they belong together. Second, the easiest, safest way to achieve clarity is by plainness: avoid frills and you can be confident you will get your meaning across without having to strain too hard.

This is why trainee journalists are instructed to write plainly: to learn to walk before they start running. And this is why style manuals that concentrate on the basics tend to elaborate Orwell's 'six elementary rules' into the Ten Commandments of Plain Writing – each one to do with keeping it simple and cutting out clutter. (*English for Journalists*, which includes a chapter on style, takes this general approach.)

The point is not that these instructions are wrong but that they are incomplete: plainness is not all. For if we distinguish between plainness and clarity, we can see that journalism – though it must have clarity – should not necessarily be plain. It should be plain where plainness is a virtue – as in basic news and instructional copy – and it should be coloured where colour is called for.

A PERSONAL STYLE

Feature writers, for example, often develop a strongly personal style – opinionated, anecdotal, gossipy. Columnists cannot do without one. They are celebrated – and paid – as much for their style as for their content. They are read because people enjoy their word play and tricks of style.

Here is A A Gill who writes about restaurants and television for the *Sunday Times*:

> Can we just get the organic thing clear? Organic does not mean additive-free; it means some additives and not others. Organic does not mean your food hasn't been washed with chemicals, frozen or kept fresh with gas, or that it has not been flown around the world. Organic does not necessarily mean it is healthier, or will make you live longer; nor does it mean tastier, fresher, or in some way improved.
>
> Organically farmed fish is not necessarily better than wild fish. Organically reared animals didn't necessarily live a happier life than non-organic ones – and their death is no less traumatic.
>
> More importantly, organic does not mean that the people who picked, packed, sowed and slaughtered were treated fairly, paid properly, or were free from artificial exploitation. The Chinese workers who drowned in Morecambe Bay were picking organic cockles for a pittance. If you really want to feed the hunger in your conscience, buy Fairtrade.
>
> So what does organic actually mean? Buggered if I know. It usually means more expensive. Whatever the original good intentions of the organic movement, their good name has been hijacked by supermarkets, bijoux delicatessens and agri-processors as a value-added designer label. Organic comes with its own basket of aspiration, snobbery, vanity and fear that retailers on tight margins can exploit. And what I mind most about it is that it has reinvigorated the old class distinction in food. There is them that have chemical-rich, force-fed battery dinner and us that have decent, healthy, caring lunch. It is the belief that you can buy not only with a clear conscience, but a colon that works like the log flume at Alton Towers.
>
> In general, I applaud and agree with many of the aims of environmentally careful producers, but it is time we all admitted that the label 'organic' has been polluted with cynicism, sentiment, sloppy practice and lies to the point where it is intellectually and practically bankrupt.
>
> And it hasn't made anyone a better cook.
> A A Gill, *Table Talk: Sweet and Sour, Salt and Bitter*, Orion, 2007

Reviewers are essentially people with opinions – the stronger the better. But a distinctive style is a great advantage because it can make a reviewer's view of the work easy to grasp and remember – as well as making the piece entertaining to read. If you read this kind of reviewer regularly, you get used to their attitudes and can more easily work out what you would think in their place.

Incidentally, there's no escaping the point that knocking review copy – like bad news – sells more papers than puffs do. Writers like Gill and Charlie Brooker of the *Guardian* are often compulsive reading in their destruction of mediocre television. Programme producers may not like it – but most readers do.

Even news stories are sometimes written to tease, intrigue and entertain as well as to inform. And while instructional copy must remain plain and simple, the sections introducing it can be anything but.

Take cookery journalism, for example: recipes must be plain, step-by-step, no frills; but the writing that introduces the recipes is often evocative, atmospheric, allusive. Before readers get down to business in the kitchen, they want to be seduced by the scent of rosemary, the softness of raspberry, the crispness of celery, while all the time the Mediterranean murmurs in the background.

THE NEW JOURNALISM

And the new journalism, meaning the adoption by mainly American journalists of various experimental techniques from the mid-1960s onwards, is the opposite of plain. For example, Tom Wolfe, pioneer and joint editor of the definitive anthology *The New Journalism*, explains his lavish use of dots, dashes, exclamation marks, italics and so on as essentially FUN:

> I found a great many pieces of punctuation and typography lying around dormant when I came along – and I must say I had a good time using them. I figured it was time someone violated what Orwell called 'the Geneva conventions of the mind' . . . a protocol that had kept journalism and non-fiction generally (and novels) in such a tedious bind for so long.

Wolfe says that he and other New Journalists – Gay Talese, Truman Capote, Terry Southern, Hunter S Thompson, Joan Didion – gradually learnt the techniques of social realism developed by novelists such as Fielding, Balzac and Dickens. They adopted such devices as realistic dialogue and scene-by-scene construction (telling the story by moving from scene to scene rather than by historical narrative).

Effectively they were claiming for journalism territory previously occupied by the novel – and repudiating the claim that journalism was somehow inferior to the novel. They were also helping to dispose of the idea that good writing is necessarily plain and simple.

Here's a snippet from a celebrated piece on the Kentucky Derby by gonzo journalist Hunter S Thompson, featuring the British cartoonist Ralph Steadman:

> I took the expressway out to the track, driving very fast and jumping the monster car back and forth between lanes, driving with a beer in one hand and my mind so muddled that I almost crushed a Volkswagen full of nuns when I swerved to catch the right exit. There was a slim chance, I thought, that I might be able to catch the ugly Britisher before he checked in.
>
> But Steadman was already in the press box when I got there, a bearded young Englishman wearing a tweed coat and HAF sunglasses. There was nothing particularly odd about him. No facial veins or clumps of bristly warts. I told him about the motel woman's description and he seemed puzzled. 'Don't let it bother you,' I said. 'Just keep in mind for the next few days that we're in Louisville, Kentucky. Not London. Not even New York. This is a weird place. You're lucky that mental defective at the motel didn't jerk a pistol out of the cash register and blow a big hole in you.' I laughed, but he looked worried.
> *Scanlan's Monthly*

'Gonzo', according to the dictionary, means 'bizarre, crazy, absurd'; is used about 'journalism of a subjective eccentric nature' – and, you might add, is certainly not politically correct. But, like the new journalism in general, this piece has life, colour and immediacy. Notice how specific it is: 'a Volkswagen full of nuns' rather than 'a carload of nuns'; 'a tweed coat and HAF sunglasses' rather than 'an overcoat and sunglasses'. Above all, it has the pace and rhythm of the spoken word. Clearly, the new journalism emphasises the continuity between speech and writing referred to above.

Earlier, the American journalist Studs Terkel developed a way of writing that took this link as far as it could be taken. His oral histories, such as *Working* and *The Good War*, are essentially edited first-person accounts. But as he once admitted, the art is in finding the natural storytellers to interview: 'You don't just bump into anyone.'

BLAME THE TAPE-RECORDER

In less talented hands writing that reproduces speech authentically can be repetitive, obscure, unstructured – in a word, unreadable. For the worst examples blame the tape-recorder and, in particular, the interviewing style known as Q&A. In what can be a travesty of journalism as an active, inquiring, interpretative process the interviewer's role seems to consist of turning the tape on and off, asking the odd question, then typing up the transcript with a minimum of editing – and in the laziest cases getting somebody else to do even that.

Here's an extract from a Q&A with a footballer, published in the monthly *French News*. As you read it you can hear the original French in which the interview was conducted:

> TN: Are you thinking of coaching in the future?
> JPP: I'm thinking of it. It needs a lot of experience.
> TN: OK, but like many other high-level sportsmen you have got the best experience on the pitch.
> JPP: Managing a team is a different matter. I'm not ready yet.
> TN: You are a 'fighter' on the ground. Is this the sort of quality you would expect from your players?
> JPP: That's obviously what I would want from them.
> TN: Why not in Bordeaux?
> JPP: Why not indeed?

And so on – ad nauseam.

WRITE BETTER THAN YOU TALK

So reproducing speech as such can't be the answer to the style question. Indeed both Robert Gunning and John Whale ('Write the way you talk'/ 'Write as you speak') hedge more than a little when they go into detail.

The Gunning message turns into: 'Actually, we recommend that writers try to write better than they talk; to eliminate pauses, repetitions of words, and too many connectives. But the goal is to achieve a conversational tone.'

And Whale expands his slogan as follows:

> By this I mean that you should try to write as you would speak if you were talking at the top of your form, unhesitantly, in the idiom that best suited your theme and the occasion, and trusting your own ear.

To which you might object: but what if I have no top form to speak of, if I can't talk coherently and unhesitantly at the same time, if my ear is wooden and I don't feel able to trust it? Does it follow that I can't become a good writer?

Pushed to the limit, the Gunning–Whale argument fails. For there are certainly people who talk badly – hesitantly, repetitively, clumsily – but manage to write well. Some successful professional writers clearly do not write as they speak.

There is another, more general problem. Most people's speech has a looser grammar than their writing: sentences change direction without warning or are left unfinished; verbs don't agree with subjects; and so on. For most people, to follow the instruction 'write as you speak' would involve either slavishly copying the loose grammar of speech or having to go through the copy afterwards to tighten up the grammar.

'Write as you speak' turns out to be an overstatement of the obvious point that good written journalism has much in common with coherent speech. To put it another way, you don't really 'write as you speak', though to write well you may spend a lot of time and energy making it look as if you do.

WRITE WITH YOUR EARS

The simplest test of writing is certainly to read it out loud. You'll know immediately if sentences are too long: you won't have the puff to finish. You should be able to hear repetitions and clumsy constructions, too.

That is negative – a matter of avoiding mistakes. More positively, you should write with what is called cadence or rhythm. For example, write sentences that build to a powerful conclusion, as this one from Dickens does:

> It was my mother, cold and dead.

Here's a more elaborate example, also from Dickens:

> Annual income twenty pounds, annual expenditure nineteen nineteen six, result happiness. Annual income twenty pounds, annual expenditure twenty pounds ought and six, result misery.

A resignation note read simply:

> Hours too long, wages too low, life too short.

With his characteristic laconic style Julius Caesar reported to Rome:

> I came, I saw, I conquered.

And Dr Johnson produced this hard drinker's motto:

> Claret is the liquor for boys; port for men; but he who aspires to be a hero must drink brandy.

Writing in triplets like this works – the third element provides a punch-line. Similarly, where there are two related points to make, try to make your sentence balance, as in this example from Hazlitt (in the *Times*):

> The love of liberty is the love of others; the love of power is the love of ourselves.

This is antithesis: contrasting two opposite points. It often uses the rhetorical device of repetition: here the word 'love' does not become 'affection' or 'passion' in the second clause; if it did, the sentence would lose its power.

The point about repetition is that it should be intentional, serving a similar function to rhyme in verse. On occasion it can run right through a section. Here's an extract from a feature published at the height of the President Clinton–Monica Lewinsky scandal in 1998:

> Let's review what we've learned so far. The president a liar? *Knew that.*
>
> The president a philanderer? *Knew that.*
>
> The president reckless in the satisfaction of his appetites? *Knew that.*
>
> The president would say anything and hurt anybody to get out of a mess? *Knew that.*
>
> Married men cheat? *Knew that.*
>
> Hillary isn't throwing Bill's stuff on the White House lawn because she is as committed to their repugnant arrangement as he is? *Knew that.*
>
> The president has the nerve to pick out a dress for a woman. *Didn't know that . . .*
> New York Times

'Knew that' runs like a chorus through the section – until we get to the punchline. Also note that 'the president' is repeated (except where Hillary comes into the story and 'Bill' is used).

There is a danger in writing with your ears: what might be called the Hiawatha effect – getting stuck in one soporific rhythm, as in:

> By the shore of Gitche Gumee
> By the shining Big-Sea-Water
> Stood the wigwam of Nokomis
> Daughter of the Moon, Nokomis . . .

Except to make a particular point (or to parody Longfellow) do not write like this: vary your rhythms.

WORDS AND PHRASES

Words and phrases are the building blocks – and the flourishes – of writing. One single powerful word can transform a paragraph:

> Say what you like about the new ITV system that has arisen from the morass of the 1990 Broadcasting Act but you can't say it doesn't cater for minorities. GMTV, for example, caters for the brain-dead, a small but important proportion of the electorate whose needs have hitherto been addressed only by Rupert Murdoch.
> *Observer*

'Brain-dead' follows an innocuous-sounding sentence – which suddenly takes on a sharper meaning.

Next, here's a gossip writer in a London glossy commenting on objections by residents to a proposed memorial garden to Diana, Princess of Wales:

> It would be easy to deride the objectors for being cold-hearted but having seen the crowds, flowers and all those public tears, one can sympathise with Kensington residents who do not wish to walk out of their front door only to trip over some grieving wretch holding a bouquet.
> *London Portrait*

A fine example of 'writing for the reader': from the pompous misuse of 'deride' (the rest of us would say something like 'criticise' or 'condemn') to the strangulated 'one' (for 'you') this has the Kensington dialect to a tee. 'Grieving wretch' is superb.

A fixation with words whether read or heard can be put to good use. Here's a bit from an interview with Gerry Adams, who admits to being nervous before speaking in public and being interviewed:

'Yes. All interviews.' Gerry Adams fixes a steady gaze, and says, slowly and deliberately, 'I urinate a lot.'

There is something very particular about the word 'urinate'. It is a term people seldom use unless they're talking to a doctor. The kind of person who chooses to tell you that they urinate when nervous is normally the type to use words like 'tinkle' or 'waterworks'. But when Adams tells me that, he does so in the pared-down bald way characteristic of people who have endured extreme physical indignity; prisoners have it, and soldiers coming back from war.
Decca Aitkenhead, *Guardian*

Or how about this?

A recent trip to America has provided me with some splendid contemporary oxymorons to add to my already huge collection. I spotted 'airline food' before I'd even landed, and an airport menu furnished two more – 'jumbo shrimp' and 'this page intentionally left blank'. . . . My favourite was observed in Los Angeles: 'police protection'.
Victor Lewis-Smith, London *Evening Standard*

Original vivid phrases are worth their weight: they stop you having to rely on the cliché. Here's one from a report on the British bodybuilding championships: the heavyweights are described as plodding on with gigantic thighs so big they impede movement . . .

. . . and buns so tight you could bounce brussels sprouts off them.
Observer

A vividly evoked picture: those huge bronzed, greased, muscular bottoms, elastically tight, and tiny green sprouts bouncing off them like squash balls – an attractively playful reaction to competitors who take themselves very seriously.

Successful phrases are often quirky, colourful, unexpected: they rely on contrast and conflict, the shock of the mismatched. For example, take a phrase and then – as though you'd landed on a snake during Snakes and Ladders – slide off somewhere surprising:

The British do not fear change. Only this morning a young man asked me for some.
Craig Brown parodying Tony Blair, *Daily Telegraph*

The only thing men get at present-giving time is bitterly disappointed.
Ms London

Or take a well-known phrase and turn it on its head:

> He was an opera fanatic, and the sort of man who gives that
> species a good name.
> Geoffrey Wheatcroft, *Opera*

> Only the young die good.
> *Anon*

Look for the unexpected, the vivid:

> 'She has Van Gogh's ear for music.'
> Alex McGregor quoting Billy Wilder, *Probe*

> Whoever writes his stuff deserves a place in Poets' Corner – as
> soon as possible.
> Russell Davies, *Daily Telegraph*

Of a Serb militiaman manning a checkpoint in Bosnia:

> If I die and go to hell, I expect him to be there at the gates.
> Martin Bell, *Observer*

Of a character in a TV play:

> A viper in peach silk and apricot satin
> Richard Williams, *Guardian*

Overstatement can work – if it is vivid and specific. Here is the American
journalist Dave Barry explaining 'Why Women Can't Play Baseball':

> Because, faced with the choice of rescuing a drowning baby and
> catching a high fly ball, a woman wouldn't hesitate to save the
> baby, even if the game was tied and there were men on base.

SENTENCES AND PARAGRAPHS

Start with the short sentence. That is: start by learning to write the short
one, then practise adding longer ones to create contrast. Like this.

The impact of a short sentence is greater if it comes before or after a long
one or several long ones. Here's a short sentence ending a paragraph:

> It was on the morning of day three that I started to worry about
> George and Rose. We were tramping through the African bush,

dutifully scanning the wilds for primeval monsters, when I suddenly noticed that George was wearing Bugs Bunny socks. *And Rose had floral shorts.* [My italics]

And here's the next par – starting with a short sentence:

Even worse, they were talking loudly. The great issue burning in their brilliant minds, as I tried to savour the incandescent glory of the African landscape, was this . . . [My italics]
Daily Telegraph

In both sentences and paragraphs the key points are the beginning and the end. As with the piece as a whole, you must get the reader's attention and then keep it. Try to begin and end with a strong word or phrase.

In general, above all with features, vary the length of your sentences. There is a place for a series of short ones – if you want to produce a breathless or staccato effect because what you're reporting is dramatic or terrible. Here, for example, is part of a quote from the fire brigade:

'The cottage is now completely gutted. Everything has gone. Only the walls are standing.'
Daily Telegraph

But there is no sense in writing a series of long sentences – unless your plan is to send the reader to sleep. Here, for example, is a paragraph of 71 words in just two sentences:

Ministers, and those they employ to whinge on their behalf, are now given to complaining that the media pay far too little attention to their achievements over the first year in office. It's an example of this Government's hypersensitivity, not to mention the ferocious rivalries within it, that I and other colleagues have been contacted by Cabinet Ministers and their functionaries over the past week with check-lists of their personal triumphs.
Observer

Political analysis seems to attract pompous and long-winded writing. In this case the sentences are long and complicated partly because the writer can't resist the aside, the parenthesis:

Ministers, and those they employ to whinge on their behalf, . . .

. . . hypersensitivity, not to mention the ferocious rivalries within it, . . .

Complete sentences, like words and phrases, are often written in threes to produce a rhetorical effect:

> Who were these people who sought to tell me what a good sunset is? Why were they invading my holiday? And how dare they defile my dusk?
> *Daily Telegraph*

FIGURES OF SPEECH

Alliteration, metaphor, simile and the rest* are part of vivid effective writing. But they can be overdone. The pun, for example, is a virus that gets into the computer systems of some tabloids.

Alliteration can be addictive. The local paper reporter who referred to 'Battersea's boxing brothers' (see page 18), which is straightforward, might not be able to resist the temptation of 'Clapham's cricketing cousins', which is clumsy and self-conscious.

And what about the *Telegraph* travel feature writer quoted above? Does his 'how dare they defile my dusk' work as a phrase? There's something awkward and forced in the combination of 'defile' and 'dusk'.

Remember that alliteration – like other forms of repetition – can be unintentional. So sometimes you need to remove it from your copy to maintain an appropriate tone, to stop a serious piece sounding comic.

TRICKS THAT DON'T WORK

As journalism has become more and more informal and colloquial, the mannerisms that might work in conversation – or even on radio – can look embarrassingly silly on the printed page. I've got no problem with slang, loose grammar, taboo words – what used to be called 'bad language' – when the context is right. I'm happy with 'And' and 'But' to start sentences. In columns and think pieces nothing beats a cunningly placed parenthesis (if only to keep the reader awake) . . . and so on.

But some 'tricks' just don't work. Here, in a piece in an upmarket news-paper about the BBC's Television Centre (and particularly the Blue Peter

---

* See *English for Journalists* for discussion of the common figures of speech.

garden) being sold off, a sentence is fatally undermined by its first few words:

> Interestingly (always a bad start to a sentence), TV Centre was designed on the back of an envelope in a pub.

This is not interesting: it is bizarre. If 'interestingly' is a bad way of starting a sentence (not much doubt about that) why not forget it and start again? Is the reader supposed to think 'Well, if the writer knows it's lousy writing, that's all right then'? As I said, bizarre.

In general, beware of expressions like 'to coin a phrase'/'as the old joke has it'/'as they say'/'forgive the cliché' when you've decided that the only way to say something is to repeat a familiar formula. Forget the apology: just go ahead and do it.

The piece quoted above included another weird example of a trick that doesn't work:

> What will happen to the Blue Peter garden, which has existed at the back of the complex since Percy Thrower, pipe-smoking darling of TV gardening, turned the first sod (which is no way to talk about John Noakes) in 1832? Sorry I mean 1974.

I'm not referring to the 1832–1974 correction, which might be a bit clumsy but isn't worth commenting on. I mean 'sod'. Either the word is a friendly, informal word like bloke (in which case there's no objection to it) or it must mean what it originally meant – 'sodomite'. And that is certainly no way to talk about John Noakes, so why do it?

TOO MANY BUTS

'But' is a powerful word. Like 'and', it has its place in journalism whether in the middle of sentences or at the beginning. But you must not overdo it.

First, avoid the false 'but', often put in to revive a flagging sentence or paragraph. Second, avoid a succession of 'buts'. Even if some of them are 'however' or 'although', the effect is to leave the reader feeling giddy. For a 'but' changes the direction of the paragraph.

> The householder could, of course, search for the owner and arrange a deal. *But* tracing an owner is a long, laborious and frustrating task

> *although* local history may give some leads. Usually, it is when no-one comes forward with a paper title (title deeds), that house-holders technically squat. *But* it can be extremely frustrating . . . [My italics]
> *Ideal Home*

Too many 'buts'.

THE IMPORTANCE OF CONTENT

A word of caution to add to this emphasis on techniques and tricks: beware of putting colour into copy in an artificial way. Style, as was said early on in this chapter, is not a matter of adding embellishment to content. It is a matter of expressing content in a lively, vivid, pleasing way.

Faced with the (usually false) choice between style and content, many great stylists would in fact choose content. Here is that caustic wit Dorothy Parker, famous for her put-downs, reviewing the autobiography of the dancer Isadora Duncan:

> *My Life* . . . is a profoundly moving book. [Isadora Duncan] was no writer, God knows. Her book is badly written, abominably written. There are passages of almost idiotic naivety and there are passages of horrendously flowery verbiage. There are veritable Hampton Court mazes of sentences. . . . There are plural pronouns airily relating to singular nouns but somehow the style of the book makes no matter. Out of this mess of prose come her hope, her passion, her suffering.
> *New Yorker*

READ, ANALYSE, PRACTISE, POLISH

To develop your writing style, you need good models. We have tried in this book to provide some examples of the kind of journalistic writing we think you should read and try to emulate.

Look for well-written books by journalists – whether collected pieces or sustained reporting. *Homage to Catalonia* shows George Orwell at his best, reporting on the Spanish Civil War. Tom Wolfe's anthology *The New Journalism* has been quoted; there are good collections by the English interviewer Lynn Barber and the American ideologue P J O'Rourke; Ian Jack's *Before the Oil Ran Out* and Bill Bryson's *Made in America* are both worth reading.

We also suggest that you read widely outside journalism: history, biography, novels. Besides the writers already mentioned – Hemingway (everything), Tom Wolfe again (particularly *Bonfire of the Vanities*), Norman Mailer (particularly *The Naked and the Dead*), Elmore Leonard and Martin Amis (*London Fields, Money*) – we would recommend Graham Greene (*The Power and the Glory, Brighton Rock, The Quiet American*), Evelyn Waugh (*Decline and Fall, Scoop*), John Steinbeck (*The Grapes of Wrath, Sweet Thursday*), P G Wodehouse (the Jeeves–Wooster books), Carson McCullers (*The Member of the Wedding, The Heart Is a Lonely Hunter*), Patricia Highsmith (the Ripley books), Peter Carey (*Oscar and Lucinda, Jack Maggs*), William Boyd (*A Good Man in Africa*), Kurt Vonnegut (*Slaughterhouse-Five*), Margery Allingham (*The Tiger in the Smoke*), Alison Lurie (*The War Between the Tates*), Sebastian Faulks (*Birdsong*) and Margaret Atwood (*The Blind Assassin*).

Second, you need to go further than mere reading. You need to analyse the pieces you read and admire, and find out for yourself how they work. We suggest you follow the approach used in this book, naming and listing different types of intros and endings, for example. Does one of them contain a technique or trick you could use in your next piece?

Third – the most obvious point – you need all the practice you can get. With it, though, you need feedback.

If you work in the kind of office where copy just disappears into a black hole with never a word from anybody about how good or bad it is, you must try to get some reaction from other people – if not colleagues in the office, friends outside it.

Finally, polish: revise your pieces, and continue to revise them even after they've been published. Go back after a while and see how they could have been improved.

When you reread something you've written, play the sub who has to read it as a bored or hostile reader would. As we said earlier, try to read your copy out loud – ideally to a friend or colleague, otherwise to yourself. This way, you're likely to spot many of the errors and problems – repetition, awkward phrasing, obscurity. You could even read your copy into a tape-recorder, then play it back.

Always remember that you are writing for your reader not yourself. So be on the lookout for those fine phrases that seem brilliant at two in the morning but lose their shine the next day. If, as advised, you find yourself having to murder your darlings, they die in a good cause.

On the other hand, if you can make your writing lively, vivid, colloquial – and clear – you will serve your reader well and encourage them to keep coming back for more.

Glossary of terms used in journalism

Journalism is rich in jargon. Some of it comes from printing (book for magazine); or survives from the pre-computer age (spike for rejected copy); or is imported from the United States (clippings for cuttings). It is often punchy and graphic (ambush, bust, fireman). But if it crops up in copy (eg in stories about the media) the sub will usually have to change it (replace 'story' by 'report') or explain it (after 'chapel' insert 'office branch' in brackets). The obvious exception is in publications for journalists such as *Press Gazette* and the *Journalist*.

ABC: Audit Bureau of Circulations – source of independently verified circulation figures
ad: advertisement
add: extra copy to add to existing story
advance: 1 text of speech or statement issued to journalists beforehand; 2 expenses paid before a trip
advertorial: advertisement presented as editorial
agencies: news agencies, eg PA and Reuters
agony column: regular advice given on personal problems sent in by readers; hence agony aunt
ambush: journalists lying in wait for unsuspecting, unwilling interviewee
ampersand: & – symbol for 'and'
angle: particular approach to story, journalist's point of view in writing it
art editor: visual journalist responsible for design and layout of publication
artwork: illustrations (eg drawings, photographs) prepared for reproduction
ascender: the part of a lower-case letter (eg b and d) that sticks out above the x-height in a typeface
attribution: identifying the journalist's source of information or quote
author's (corrections, marks): proof corrections by writer of story

back number, issue: previous issue of publication
back of the book: second part of magazine (after the centre spread)
backbench, the: senior newspaper journalists who make key production decisions

backgrounder: explanatory feature to accompany news story

bad break: clumsy hyphenation at the end of a line

banner (headline): one in large type across front page

basket: where copy goes – once a physical basket, now a digital folder

bastard measure: type set to a width that is not standard for the page

beard: the space between a letter and the edge of the base on which it is designed

beat: American term for specialist area covered by reporter

bill(board): poster promoting edition of newspaper, usually highlighting main news story

black: duplicate of written story (from colour of carbon paper once used with typewriter)

bleed: (of an image) go beyond the type area to the edge of a page

blob: solid black circle used for display effect or to tabulate lists

blob par: extra paragraph introduced by blob

blow up: enlarge (part of) photograph

blown quote: another term for pull quote

blurb: displayed material promoting contents of another page or future issue

body copy: the main text of a story, as opposed to page furniture

body type: the main typeface in which a story is set (as opposed to display)

bold: thick black type, used for emphasis

book: printer's (and so production journalist's) term for magazine

bot: black on tone

box: copy enclosed by rules to give it emphasis and/or separate it from the main text

breaker: typographical device, eg crosshead, used to break up text on the page

brief: 1 short news item; 2 instruction to journalist on how to approach story

bring up: bring forward part of story to earlier position

broadsheet: large-format newspaper

bromide: photographic print

bullet (point): another term for blob

bureau: office of news agency or newspaper office in foreign country

business-to-business (b2b): current term for what were once called 'trade' magazines, ie those covering a business area, profession, craft or trade

bust: (of a headline) be too long for the space available

buy-up interview: exclusive bought by publication

byline: writer's name as it appears in print at the beginning of a story

c & lc: capital and lower-case letters

call out: another term for pull quote

calls (also check calls): routine phone calls made by reporters to organisations such as police and fire brigade to see if a story is breaking

camera-ready: (eg artwork) prepared for reproduction

caps: capital letters

caption: words used with a picture (usually underneath), identifying where necessary and relating it to the accompanying story

caption story: extension of picture caption into a self-contained story

cast off: estimate amount of printed matter copy would make

casual: journalist employed by the shift

catch(line): short word (not printed) identifying different elements of a story in the editorial process

centre: set type with equal space on either side

centre spread: middle opening of tabloid or magazine

chapel: office branch of media union (the shop steward is the father, FoC, or mother, MoC, of the chapel)

character: unit of measurement for type including letters, figures, punctuation marks and spaces

chequebook journalism: paying large sums for stories

chief sub: senior subeditor in charge of the others

city desk: financial section of British national newspaper (in the US the city desk covers home news)

classified advertising: small ads 'classified' by subject matter, grouped in a separate section

clippings/clips: American term for cuttings

close quotes: end of section in direct quotes

close up: reduce space between lines, words or characters

CMYK: cyan, magenta, yellow and black, the process (basic printing) colours

col: column

colour piece: news story written as feature with emphasis on journalist's reactions

colour sep(aration)s: method by which the four process colours (CMYK) are separated from a colour original

column: 1 standard vertical division of page; 2 regular feature by journalist often encouraged to be opinionated and/or entertaining

column rule: light rule between columns of type

conference: meeting of editorial staff to plan current/next issue

consumer magazines: the category includes specialist titles (eg *Angling Times*), women's magazines and those of general interest

contact sheet: photographer's sheet of small prints

contacts book: a journalist's list of contacts with details of phone, fax, email, etc

contents bill: *see* bill

controlled circulation: free distribution of specialist title to target readership by geography (free newspapers) or interest group (business-to-business magazines)

copy: text of story

copy taster: *see* taster

copyright: right to reproduce original material

copytaker: telephone typist who takes down copy from reporter

corr: correspondent

correction: published statement correcting errors in story

correspondent: journalist covering specialist area, eg education

coverlines: selling copy on front cover

credit (line): name of photographer or illustrator as it appears in print next to their work

Cromalins: the Dupont system of glossy colour proofs
crop: cut (image) to size or for better effect
crosshead: line or lines, taken from the text, set bigger and bolder than the body type and inserted between paragraphs to liven up page
cut: shorten or delete copy
cut-out: illustration with background masked, painted or cut to make it stand out on the page
cuts: cuttings
cuttings: stories taken (originally cut) from newspapers and filed electronically under subject
cuttings job: story that is over-dependent on cuttings

dateline: place from which copy is filed
deadline: time story (or any part of it) is due
deck: originally one of a series of headlines stacked on top of each other; now usually used to mean one line of a headline
delayed drop: device in news story of delaying important facts for effect
delete: remove
descender: the part of a lower-case letter (eg g and j) that sticks out below the x-height in a typeface
desk: newspaper department, eg picture desk
deskman: American term for male subeditor
diary, the: list of news events to be covered; hence an off-diary story is one originated by the reporter
diary column: gossip column
direct input: transmission of copy direct from the journalist's keyboard to the computer for typesetting (as opposed to the old system in which compositors retyped copy)
disclaimer: statement explaining that a particular person or organisation was not the subject of a previously published story
display ads: ordinary (not 'classified') ads which appear throughout a publication
display type: type for headlines, etc
district reporter: one covering a particular area away from the main office
doorstepping: reporters lying in wait for (usually) celebrities outside their homes
double: a story published twice in the same issue of a publication
double-column: (of text, headline, illustration) across two columns
double (page) spread: two facing pages in a magazine, whether advertising or editorial
downtable subs: those other than the chief sub and deputies
drop cap, letter: outsize initial capital letter used to start story or section; it drops down alongside the text which is indented to accommodate it
drop quotes: outsize quotes used to mark quoted matter
dummy: 1 pre-publication edition of new publication used to sell advertising and experiment editorially; 2 blank version of publication, eg to show quality and weight of paper; 3 complete set of page proofs

edition: version of newspaper printed for particular circulation area or time

editor: senior journalist responsible for publication or section

editorial: 1 leading article expressing editorial opinion; 2 content that is not advertising

editor's conference: main planning meeting for next issue

em, en: units of measurement for type – the width of the two letters m and n

embargo: time before which an organisation supplying material, eg by press release, does not want it published

ends: the story ends here

EPD: electronic picture desk

EPS file: Encapsulated PostScript file

exclusive: claim by publication that it has a big story nobody else has

exes: journalists' out-of-pocket expenses

face: type design

facing matter: (of advertising) opposite editorial

facsimile: exact reproduction, as with electronic transmission of pages

feature: article that goes beyond reporting of facts to explain and/or entertain; also used of any editorial matter that is not news or listings; hence feature writer, features editor

file: transmit copy

filler: short news item to fill space

fireman: traditional term for reporter sent to trouble spot when story breaks

fit: (of copy, etc) to occupy exactly the space available

flannel panel: magazine's address, contact information and list of staff

flash: brief urgent message from news agency

flatplan: page-by-page plan of issue

flip: (of picture) transpose left to right

flush left or right: (of type) having one consistent margin with the other ragged

fold, the: centre fold in a newspaper so that only the upper half of the paper ('above the fold') is visible at the point of sale

folio: page (number)

follow up: take published story as the starting point for an update

format: 1 size, shape or style of publication or section; 2 computer instruction; hence to format

fount (pronounced font and now often spelt that way): typeface

free(sheet): free newspaper

freebie: something useful or pleasant, often a trip, supplied free to journalists

freelance: self-employed journalist who sells material to various outlets

freelancer: American term for freelance

fudge: another term for stop press

full out: (of type) not indented

galley proof: typeset proof not yet made up into a page

gatefold: an extra page which folds out from a magazine

ghost writer: journalist writing on behalf of someone else, often by interviewing them; hence to ghost (eg a column)

gone to bed: passed for press so too late for corrections

grams per square metre (gsm; g/m2): the measure used to define the weight of paper
graphics: visual material, usually drawn
grid: design skeleton specifying (eg) number and width of columns
gutter: space between two facing pages; can also be used of space between columns

H & J: (of copy on screen) hyphenated and justified, so in the form in which it will be typeset
hack, hackette: jocular terms for journalist
hair space: thinnest space between typeset letters
half-tone: illustration broken into dots of varying sizes
handout: printed material, eg press release, distributed to journalists
hanging indent: copy set with first line of each paragraph full out and subsequent ones indented
hard copy: copy on paper, eg printout, rather than screen
head, heading: headline
heavy: broadsheet newspaper
heavy type: thicker than standard
hold (over): keep material for future use
hot metal: old typesetting system in which type was cast from molten metal
house ad: publisher's advertisement in its own publication
house journal: publication for employees of a particular organisation
house style: the way a publication chooses to publish in matters of detail

imposition: arrangement of pages for printing
imprint: name and address of publisher and printer
in-house: inside a media organisation
in pro: in proportion (used of visual material to be reduced)
indent: set copy several characters in from left-hand margin
input: type copy into computer
insert: 1 extra copy to be included in existing story; 2 printed matter inserted in publication after printing and binding
intro: first paragraph of story; also used (confusingly) in some magazine offices to mean standfirst
ISDN: integrated services digital network – a means of transmitting editorial material between offices, to printers, etc
italics: italic (sloping) type

jackline: another word for widow
journo: jocular term for journalist
justified: type set with consistent margins

kern: reduce the space between characters in typeset copy
kicker: introductory part of caption or headline
kill: drop a story; hence kill fee for freelance whose commissioned story is not used
knocking copy: story written with negative angle

label: (of headline) without a verb

landscape: horizontal picture

layout: arrangement of body type, headlines, etc and illustrations on the page

lead: 1 main story on a page; 2 tip-off or idea for story (in the US the intro of a story is called the lead)

leader: leading article expressing editorial opinion

leader dots: three dots used to punctuate

leading (pronounced 'ledding'): space between lines (originally made by inserting blank slugs of lead between lines of type)

leg: column of typeset copy

legal: send material to be checked for legal problems, eg libel

legal kill: lawyer's instruction not to use

lensman: American term for male photographer

letter spacing: space between letters

libel: defamatory statement in permanent or broadcast form

lift: 1 use all or most of a story taken from one newspaper edition in the next; 2 steal a story from another media outlet and reproduce it with few changes

ligature: two or more joined letters

light face: type lighter than standard

linage (this spelling preferred to lineage): payment to freelances by the line; also refers to classifed advertising without illustration

line drawing: drawing made up of black strokes

listings: lists of entertainment and other events with basic details

literal: typographical error

lobby, the: specialist group of political reporters covering parliament

local corr: local correspondent

logo: name, title or recognition word in particular design used on regular section or column; also used of magazine's front-page title

lower case: ordinary letters (not caps)

make-up: assembly of type and illustrations on the page ready for reproduction

mark up: specify the typeface, size and width in which copy is to be set

masking: covering part of photograph for reproduction

masthead: publication's front-page title

measure: width of typesetting

medium type: between light and heavy

merchandising: details of stockists and prices in consumer features

mf: more copy follows

model release: contract signed by photographic model authorising use of pictures

mono(chrome): printed in one colour, usually black

more: more copy follows

mug shot: photograph showing head (and sometimes shoulders)

must: copy that must appear, eg apology or correction

mutton: old name for an em

neg: photographic negative
news agency: supplier of news and features to media outlets
news desk: organising centre of newsroom
newsman: American term for male reporter
newsprint: standard paper on which newspapers are printed
newsroom: news reporters' room
nib: news in brief – short news item
night lawyer: barrister who reads newspaper proofs for legal problems
nose: intro of story; hence to renose – rewrite intro
NUJ: National Union of Journalists
nut: old name for an en; hence nutted, type indented one en

obit: obituary
off-diary: *see* diary, the
off-the-record: statements made to a journalist on the understanding that they will not be reported directly or attributed
on spec: uncommissioned (material submitted by freelance)
on-the-record: statements made to a journalist that can be reported and attributed
op-ed: feature page facing page with leading articles
open quotes: start of section in direct quotes
originals: photographs or other visual material for reproduction
orphan: first line of a paragraph at the foot of a page or column
out take: another term for pull quote
overlay: sheet of transparent paper laid over artwork with instructions on how to process it
overline: another word for strapline
overmatter: typeset material that does not fit the layout and must be cut
overprint: print over a previously printed background

PA: Press Association, Britain's national news agency
package: main feature plus sidebars
page furniture: displayed type, eg headlines, standfirsts and captions, used to project copy
page plan: editorial instructions for layout
page proof: proof of a made-up page
pagination: the number of pages in a publication; also a newspaper system's ability to make up pages
panel: another word for box
par, para: paragraph
paparazzo/i: photographer(s) specialising in pursuing celebrities
paste-up: page layout pasted into position
patch: specialist area covered by reporter
pay-off: final twist or flourish in the last paragraph of a story
peg: reason for publishing feature at a particular time
photomontage: illustration created by combining several photographs
pic, pix: press photograph(s)
pica: unit of type measurement

pick-up (of photographs): those that already exist and can therefore be picked up by journalists covering a story

picture desk: organising centre of collection and editing of pictures

piece: article

plate: printing image carrier from which pages are printed

point: 1 full stop; 2 standard unit of type size

pool: group of reporters sharing information and releasing it to other media organisations

PostScript: Adobe's page description language

PR(O): public relations (officer); hence someone performing a public relations role

press cuttings: *see* cuttings

press release: written announcement or promotional material by organisation sent to media outlets and individual journalists

profile: portrait in words of individual or organisation

proof: printout of part or whole of page so it can be checked and corrected

proofread: check proofs; hence proofreader

publisher: 1 publishing company; 2 individual in magazine publishing company with overall responsibility for title or group of titles

puff: story promoting person or organisation

pull: proof; to pull is to take a proof

pull (out) quote (blown quote, call out, out take): short extract from text set in larger type as part of page layout

pullout: separate section of publication that can be pulled out

pyramid: (usually inverted) conventional structure for news story with most important facts in intro

query: question mark

queue: collection of stories held in a computer

quote: verbatim quotation

quotes: quotation marks

ragged: (of type) with uneven margin

raised cap: outsize initial capital letter used to start story or section; it is raised above the text

range left or right: (of type) have one consistent margin with the other ragged

register: alignment of coloured inks on the printed page

rejig: rewrite copy, particularly in the light of later information

renose: rewrite intro of a story

reporter: gatherer and writer of news

repro house: company that processes colour pictures ready for printing

retainer: regular payment to local correspondent or freelance

retouch: alter photograph to emphasise particular feature

Reuters: international news agency

reverse indent: another term for hanging indent

reversed out: (type) printed in white on black or tinted background

revise: extra proof to check that corrections have been made

rewrite: write new version of story or section as opposed to subbing on copy

ring-round: story based on series of phone calls
river: white space running down a column of type, caused by space between
   words
roman: plain upright type
rough: sketch for layout
round-up: gathering of disparate elements for single story
RSI: repetitive strain injury, attributed to overuse and misuse of computer
   keyboard, mouse, etc
rule: line between columns or round illustrations
run: period of printing an edition or number of copies printed
run on: (of type) continue from one line, column or page to the next
running foot: title and issue date at the foot of the page
running head: title and issue date at the top of the page
running story: one that is constantly developing, over a newspaper's different
   editions or a number of days
running turns: pages with no paragraph breaks on first and last lines; also
   used of columns
rush: second most urgent message from news agency (after flash)

sans (serif): plain type (*see* serif) – this is an example
scaling (of pictures): calculating depth
schedule: 1 list of jobs for (eg) reporters; 2 publication's printing programme
scheme: make a plan of page layout
scoop: jocular word for exclusive
screamer: exclamation mark
screen: the number of dots per square inch of a half-tone
section: 1 separately folded part of newspaper; 2 complete printed sheet
   making up part of magazine
sell: another word for standfirst, often used in women's magazines
serif: decorative addition to type – this is an example of serif type
set and hold: typeset and keep for use later
setting: copy set in type
shift: daily stint worked by staff journalists and casuals
shoot: a photographic session
shy: (of headline) too short for the space available
sidebar: subsidiary story or other material placed next to main story, usually
   in box
sidehead: subsidiary heading, set flush left
sign-off: writer's name as it appears in print at the end of a story
sketch: light-hearted account of events, especially parliamentary
slip: newspaper edition for particular area or event
small caps: capital letters in smaller size of the same typeface
snap: early summary by news agency of important story to come
snapper: jocular term for press photographer
snaps: press photographs
solid: (of type) set without extra leading
spike: where rejected copy goes (originally a metal spike)
splash: newspaper's main front-page story

splash sub: subeditor responsible for tabloid's front page
spoiler: attempt by newspaper to reduce impact of rival's exclusive by publishing similar story
spot colour: second colour (after black) used in printing publication
spread: two facing pages
s/s: same size
standfirst: introductory matter accompanying headline, particularly used in features
stet: ignore deletion or correction (Latin for 'let it stand')
stone: bench where pages were made up; hence stone sub – subeditor who makes final corrections and cuts on page proofs
stop press: small area on back page of newspaper left blank for late news in days of hot metal
story: article, especially news report
strap(line): subsidiary headline above main headline
Street, the: Fleet Street, where many newspapers once had their offices
stringer: local correspondent; freelance on contract to a news organisation
style: house style
style book/style sheet: where house style is recorded
sub: subeditor
subhead: subsidiary headline
subtitle: another word for standfirst

tab(loid): popular small-format newspaper such as the *Sun*
tagline: explanatory note under headline
take: section of copy for setting
take back: (on proof) take words back to previous line
take over: (on proof) take words forward to next line
taster: production journalist who checks and selects copy; also coverline
think piece: feature written to show and provoke thought
tie-in: story connected with the one next to it
tint: shaded area on which type can be printed
tip(-off): information supplied (and usually paid for) whether by freelance or member of the public
titlepiece: traditional term for name of magazine as it appears on the cover – now replaced by masthead and logo
TOT: triumph over tragedy, feature formula particularly popular in women's magazines
tracking: space between characters
trade names: product names (eg Hoover, Kleenex, Velcro)
tranny: transparency – photograph in film form
trans(pose): reverse order
turn: part of story continued on a later page
typeface: a complete range of type in a particular style, eg Times New Roman
typescale: measuring rule for type
typo: American term for typographical error
typography: craft of using type

u/lc: upper and lower case
underscore: underline
unj(ustified): text set flush left, ragged right
upper and lower case: mixture of capitals and ordinary letters
upper case: capital letters

vignette: illustration whose edges gradually fade to nothing
vox pop: series of street interviews (Latin: *vox populi* – voice of the people)

weight: thickness or boldness of letters in a typeface
white space: area on page with no type or illustration
widow: single word or part of word at the end of a paragraph on a line by
    itself; originally the last line of a paragraph at the top of a page or column
wire: a means of transmitting copy by electronic signal; hence wire room
wob: white on black – type reversed out
wot: white on tone

x-height: height of the lower-case letters of a typeface (excluding ascenders
    and descenders)

Further reading

ENGLISH USAGE AND WRITING STYLE

Amis, Kingsley, *The King's English*, HarperCollins, 1997

Blamires, Harry, *Correcting your English*, Bloomsbury, 1996

Bryson, Bill, *Troublesome Words*, Viking, 2001

Burchfield, R W (ed.), *The New Fowler's Modern English Usage* (third edition), OUP, 1996

Burridge, Kate, *Blooming English*, ABC Books for the Australian Broadcasting Corporation, 2002

Cochrane, James, *Between You and I*, Icon, 2003

Dummett, Michael, *Grammar and Style for Examination Candidates and Others*, Duckworth, 1993

Evans, Harold, *Essential English for Journalists, Editors and Writers*, revised by Crawford Gillan, Pimlico, 2000

Gowers, Sir Ernest, *The Complete Plain Words* (second edition), revised by Sir Bruce Fraser, Pelican, 1977

Greenbaum, Sidney, and Whitcut, Janet, *Longman Guide to English Usage*, Penguin, 1996

Hicks, Wynford, *English for Journalists* (third edition), Routledge, 2007

—— *Quite Literally: Problem Words and How to Use Them*, Routledge, 2004

Humphrys, John, *Lost for Words*, Hodder, 2005

Mayes, Ian, *Only Correct: The Best of Corrections & Clarifications*, Guardian, 2005

Partridge, Eric, *You Have a Point There*, Routledge, 1990

—— *Usage and Abusage* (third edition), revised by Janet Whitcut, Penguin, 1999

Strunk, William, *The Elements of Style* (third edition), revised by E B White, Macmillan (New York), 1979, also available free at www.bartleby.com/141/

Trask, R L, *Mind the Gaffe*, Penguin, 2001

Truss, Lynne, *Eats, Shoots & Leaves*, Profile, 2003

Waterhouse, Keith, *Waterhouse on Newspaper Style*, Viking, 1989

—— *English Our English*, Viking, 1991

HOUSE STYLE

Austin, Tim (comp) *The Times Style and Usage Guide*, Collins, 2003
  (updated online edition: www.timesonline.co.uk)
The Economist Style Guide (eighth edition), Economist, 2003
Marsh, David, *Guardian Style*, Guardian, 2007 (updated online edition: www.
  guardian.co.uk)
Ritter, R M (ed. and comp.), *The Oxford Dictionary for Writers and Editors*
  (second edition), OUP, 2000

PRINT JOURNALISM SKILLS

Adams, Sally, *Interviewing for Journalists*, Routledge, 2001
Frost, Chris, *Reporting for Journalists*, Routledge, 2001
Hicks, Wynford, and Holmes, Tim, *Subediting for Journalists*, Routledge, 2002
Keeble, Richard, *Ethics for Journalists*, Routledge, 2001
McNae's Essential Law for Journalists, latest edition, Butterworths
Mason, Peter, and Smith, Derrick, *Magazine Law*, Routledge, 1998

NON-FICTION BY JOURNALISTS

This section includes collections and books about journalism.

Let Us Now Praise Famous Men is classic reporting from the 1930s about three
  Alabama share-croppers – impoverished cotton farmers. *The Years with Ross* is
  a memoir of New Yorker editor Harold Ross.

Agee, James, and Evans, Walker, *Let Us Now Praise Famous Men*, Houghton
  Mifflin, 1991
Amis, Martin, *The Moronic Inferno*, Penguin, 1987
Barber, Lynn, *Demon Barber*, Viking, 1998
Bernstein, Carl, and Woodward, Bob, *All the President's Men*, Pocket Books,
  1994
Bryson, Bill, *Made in America*, Minerva, 1995
Carter, Angela, *Nothing Sacred*, Virago, 1982
Coleman, Nick, and Hornby, Nick, *The Picador Book of Sports Writing*, Picador,
  1997
Evans, Harold, *Good Times, Bad Times*, Phoenix, 1994
Harris, Robert, *Selling Hitler*, Arrow, 1996
Jack, Ian, *Before the Oil Ran Out*, Fontana, 1988
Mitford, Jessica, *The Making of a Muckraker*, Quartet, 1980, out of print
O'Rourke, P J, *Holidays in Hell*, Picador, 1989
—— *Parliament of Whores*, Picador, 1992
Orwell, George, *The Collected Essays, Journalism and Letters of George Orwell*, vols
  I–IV, ed. Sonia Orwell and Ian Angus, Penguin, 1970
—— *Homage to Catalonia*, Penguin, 1989

Silvester, Christopher, ed., *The Penguin Book of Interviews*, Viking, 1993
—— *The Penguin Book of Columnists*, Viking, 1997
Terkel, Studs, *Working*, Penguin, 1985
Thurber, James, *The Years with Ross*, Penguin, 1963, out of print
Wolfe, Tom, and Johnson, E W, *The New Journalism*, Picador, 1990

REFERENCE FOR REVIEWERS

Art

Murray, Peter, and Murray Linda, *The Penguin Dictionary of Art and Artists*,
    Penguin, seventh edition, 1997
Osborne, Harold, *The Oxford Companion to Art*, Oxford University Press,
    1970

Books

Drabble, Margaret, ed., *The Oxford Companion to English Literature*, Oxford
    University Press, fifth edition, 1998
Sturrock, John, ed., *The Oxford Guide to Contemporary Writing*, Oxford University
    Press, 1996

Dance

Clarke, Mary, and Crisp, Clement, *London Contemporary Dance Theatre: The
    First Twenty-One Years*, Dance Books, 1988
Koegler, Horst, ed., *The Concise Oxford Dictionary of Ballet*, Oxford University
    Press, second edition, 1982

Film

Katz, Ephraim, *The Macmillan International Film Encyclopedia*, Macmillan, second
    edition, 1994
Walker John, ed., *Halliwell's Film and Video Guide*, HarperCollins, thirteenth
    edition, 1998

Music

Broughton, Simon, Ellingham, Mark, Muddyman, David, and Trilloe, Richard,
    eds, *The Rough Guide to World Music*, The Rough Guides, 1994
Clarke, Donald, ed., *The Penguin Encyclopedia of Popular Music*, Viking, second
    edition, 1998

Sadie, Stanley, ed., *The New Grove Dictionary of Music and Musicians*, Grove, 1997

Opera

Harewood, Earl of, and Peattie, Anthony, eds, *The New Kobbé's Opera Book*, Ebury Press, eleventh edition, 1997

Television

Gambaccini, Paul, *Television's Greatest Hits: Every Hit Television Programme Since 1960*, Network Books, 1993
Hayward, Anthony, *Who's Who on Television*, Boxtree, 1998
Vahimagi, Tise, *British Television: An Illustrated Guide*, Oxford University Press, 1996

Theatre

Hartnoll, Phyllis, *The Oxford Companion to the Theatre*, Oxford University Press, fourth edition, 1983

Index

Related titles in the Media Skills series

English for Journalists
Third Edition

Wynford Hicks

Praise for previous editions:

'For those uncertain of their word power and those who know in their bones that they are struggling along on waffle, a couple of hours with this admirably written manual would be time well spent.'
Keith Waterhouse, *British Journalism Review*

'*English for Journalists* is a jolly useful book. It's short. It's accessible. It's cheap. And it tells you what you want to know.'
Humphrey Evans, *Journalist*

'It makes a simple-to-use guide that you could skim read on a train journey or use as a basic textbook that you can dip into to solve specific problems.'
Short Words

English for Journalists is an invaluable guide not only to the basics of English, but to those aspects of writing, such as reporting speech, house style and jargon, which are specific to the language of journalism.

Written in an accessible style, *English for Journalists* covers the fundamentals of grammar, the use of spelling, punctuation and journalistic writing, with each point illustrated by concise examples.

This revised and updated edition includes:

- an introductory chapter which discusses the present state of English and current trends in journalistic writing
- a new chapter in the grammar section featuring 10 of the most common howlers made by journalists
- up-to-date examples of spelling, punctuation and usage mistakes published in newspapers and magazines
- a specimen house-style guide reproduced in full
- an extended glossary of terms used in journalism

ISBN10: 0–415–40419–3 (hbk)
ISBN10: 0–415–40420–7 (pbk)
ISBN10: 0–203–96766–6 (ebk)

ISBN13: 978–0–415–40419–8 (hbk)
ISBN13: 978–0–415–40420–4 (pbk)
ISBN13: 978–0–203–96766–9 (ebk)

Available at all good bookshops
For ordering and further information please visit:
www.routledge.com

Related titles in the Media Skills series

Ethics for Journalists
Richard Keeble

'Richard Keeble's book asks questions which dominate our working lives and it is invaluable not just to working journalists and students, but to the reading and listening public on whom our work depends.

There isn't a journalist who would not benefit from reading this book especially if he or she attempts to answer some of the questions in it.'
Paul Foot

Ethics for Journalists tackles many of the issues which journalists face in their everyday lives – from the media's supposed obsession with sex, sleaze and sensationalism, to issues of regulation and censorship. Its accessible style and question and answer approach highlights the relevance of ethical issues for everyone involved in journalism, both trainees and professionals, whether working in print, broadcast or new media.

Ethics for Journalists provides a comprehensive overview of ethical dilemmas and features interviews with a number of journalists, including the celebrated correspondent Phillip Knightely. Presenting a range of imaginative strategies for improving media standards and supported by a thorough bibliography and a wide ranging list of websites, *Ethics for Journalists* considers many problematic subjects including:

- the representation of women, blacks, gays and lesbians, and the mentally ill
- controversial calls for a privacy law to restrain the power of the press
- journalistic techniques such as sourcing the news, doorstepping, deathknocks and the use of subterfuge
- the impact of competition, ownership and advertising on media standards
- the handling of confidential sources and the dilemmas of war reporting

ISBN10: 0–415–24296–7 (hbk)
ISBN10: 0–415–24297–5 (pbk)
ISBN10: 0–203–18197–2 (ebk)

ISBN13: 978–0–415–24296–7 (hbk)
ISBN13: 978–0–415–24297–4 (pbk)
ISBN13: 978–0–203–18197–3 (ebk)

Available at all good bookshops
For ordering and further information please visit:
www.routledge.com

Related titles in the Media Skills series

Interviewing for Journalists

Sally Adams with Wynford Hicks

Interviewing for Journalists details the central journalistic skill of how to ask the right question in the right way. It is a practical and concise guide for all print journalists – professionals, students and trainees – whether writing news stories or features for newspapers or periodicals.

Interviewing for Journalists focuses on the many types of interviewing, from the routine street interview, vox pop and press conference to the interview used as the basis of an in-depth profile. Drawing on previously published material and featuring interviews with a number of successful columnists such as Lynda Lee-Potter of the Daily Mail and Andrew Duncan of Radio Times, *Interviewing for Journalists* covers every stage of interviews including research, planning and preparation, structuring questions, the vital importance of body language, how to get a vivid quote, checking material and editing it into different formats.

Interviewing for Journalists includes:

- A discussion about the significance and importance of the interview for journalism
- Advice on how to handle different interviewees such as politicians, celebrities and vulnerable people
- How to carry out the telephone interview
- Tips on note-taking and recording methods including shorthand
- A discussion of ethical, legal and professional issues such as libel, doorstepping, off-the-record briefings and the limits of editing
- A glossary of journalistic terms and notes on further reading

ISBN10: 0–415–22913–8 (hbk)
ISBN10: 0–415–22914–6 (pbk)
ISBN10: 0–203–99607–0 (ebk)

ISBN13: 978–0–415–22913–5 (hbk)
ISBN13: 978–0–415–22914–2 (pbk)
ISBN13: 978–0–203–99607–2 (ebk)

Available at all good bookshops
For ordering and further information please visit:
www.routledge.com

Related titles in the Media Skills series

Subediting for Journalists
Wynford Hicks & Tim Holmes

Subediting for Journalists is a concise, up-to-date and readable introduction to the skills of subediting for newspapers and magazines. It describes how subediting has developed, from the early days of printing to the modern era of computers and the internet, and explains clearly what the sub now has to do.

Using practical examples from newspapers and magazines, *Subediting for Journalists* introduces the various techniques involved in subediting, from cutting copy to writing captions and cover lines.

Subediting for Journalists includes:

- house style explained with a model stylebook provided
- examples of bad journalistic English
- subbing news and features for sense and style
- editing quotes and reader letters
- writing headlines and standfirsts
- making copy legally safe
- understanding production, using software packages and website subbing

ISBN10: 0–415–24084–0 (hbk)
ISBN10: 0–415–24085–9 (pbk)

ISBN13: 978–0–415–24084–0 (hbk)
ISBN13: 978–0–415–24085–7 (pbk)

Available at all good bookshops
For ordering and further information please visit:
www.routledge.com

Related titles in the Media Skills series

Writing for Broadcast Journalists

Rick Thompson

Writing for Broadcast Journalists guides readers through the differences between written and spoken language in journalism, helping broadcast journalists at every stage of their career to steer past such pitfalls as pronunciation, terms of address, and Americanised phrases, as well as to capitalise on the immediacy of the spoken word in writing broadcast news scripts.

Written in a lively and accessible style by an experienced BBC radio and TV journalist, *Writing for Broadcast Journalists* provides an invaluable guide to the techniques of writing for radio, television and online news sources.

Sections include:

- guidance on tailoring your writing style to suit a particular broadcast news audience
- advice on editing agency copy
- tips on how to avoid clichés, 'news-speak' and Americanisms
- an appendix of 'dangerous' words and phrases, explaining correct usage and advising when to avoid certain terms.

ISBN10: 0–415–31796–7 (hbk)
ISBN10: 0–415–31797–5 (pbk)
ISBN10: 0–203–34267–4 (ebk)

ISBN13: 978–0–415–31796–2 (hbk)
ISBN13: 978–0–415–31797–9 (pbk)
ISBN13: 978–0–203–34267–1 (ebk)

Available at all good bookshops
For ordering and further information please visit:
www.routledge.com